Mark the Music

For Estelle,
with great admiration for
you and your work,
warmly
Menuhin
Dec 2012

The man that hath no music in himself,
Nor is not moved with concord of sweet sounds,
Is fit for treasons, stratagems, and spoils;
The motions of his spirit are dull as night
And his affections dark as Erebus:
Let no such man be trusted. Mark the music.

Shakespeare, *The Merchant of Venice*

Mark the Music

POEMS

≈

MERRILL LEFFLER

DRYAD PRESS ▌▌ WASHINGTON, D.C.

The paper used in this publication meets the minimum requirement of American National Standard for Information Sciences — Permanence of paper for Printed Library Materials, ANSIZ39.48

Yiddish typography (pp. 74 and 120) by Yankl Salant, Graphic, Editorial and Translation Services
Hebrew typography (pp. 41 and 77) by Moshe Dor

Book and cover design by Sandy Rodgers

Library of Congress Cataloging-in-Publication Data

Leffler, Merrill, 1941-
  Mark the music : poems / by Merrill Leffler.
     p. cm.
  Includes bibliographical references.
  ISBN 978-1-928755-14-2 (alk. paper)
  I. Title.
  PS3562.E378M37   2012
  811'.54–dc23   2012006925

DRYAD PRESS
P.O. Box 11233
Takoma Park, Maryland 20912
www.dryadpress.com

This book is dedicated with love to
Ann, Jeremy, Daniel, and Sabine
and the three graces
Sophie, Johanna, Ella

Contents

Acknowledgments

Thanks to the editors of the publications where these poems first appeared, sometimes in different forms:

Kim Roberts and *Beltway*: "Morning Talk in the Branches," "Dismantling," "Morning — Early Summer"; "The Indefatigable It," "Sparrow," "Performance"; Rodger Kamenetz and *Forward*: "What We Want of It" (section 1); *Ha'Dor*: Moshe Dor translations into Hebrew of "A Short History" and "Take Hold"; Greg McBride and *Innisfree*: "Under a Full Moon at Midnight," "The Past," "The Republic of Imperishable Lines"; *Moment Magazine*: "Suite" (part 3); Grace Cavalieri and *Ocho 23*: "Arise," "Failure," "Stories," "Rejoice," "Ah!"; Shelby Stephenson and *Pembroke*: "How, You Ask, Does It Contribute to Heightening the Effectiveness of What Is Going On?" (retitled "The Indefatigable It"), "Limits" (published as "from Alive"); Herman Taube translations into Yiddish, *Der Onhoyb*; *Poet Lore*: "What We Want of It" (section 2); *The Montserrat Review*: "The Maw of Art"; Marc Steven Dworkin and *Shirim* — A Jewish Poetry Journal: "Around," "The Rain Is Ready to Fall," "The Wind Grinds"; Eric Bond and *The Takoma Voice*: "Roscoe of Takoma Park"; *Tikkun*: "Children / Yeladim"; *Voices — The Art and Science of Psychotherapy*: "The Storied Past" and "WPSY Streaming"; *William Stafford Newsletter*: "Breakfast."

Anthologies: *Cabin Fever — Poets at Joaquin Miller's Cabin*, 1984-2001: "Farewell"; *Full Moon on K Street: Poems about Washington*, ed. Kim Roberts: "Morning — Early Summer"; *Open Door — A Poet Lore Anthology 1980-1996*, eds. Philip K. Jason, Barbara Goldberg, Geraldine Connolly, Roland Flint: "Metaphor"; *The Poet's Cookbook — Recipes from Germany*," eds. Grace Cavalieri and Sabine Pascarelli: "Frühstück," translated by Sabine Pascarelli.

Several poems were first published, in different forms, in *Partly Pandemonium, Partly Love* and *Take Hold*.

I want to thank Henry Allen for his haunted portrait; Ann Slayton for making her way through various stages of the manuscript and for her always forthright eye and ear; friends who have been generous with critical attention: Herman Taube, Myra Sklarew, Grace Cavalieri, Dan Herman, Barbara Goldberg, Jack Greer, and Jean Nordhaus. Finally to Sandy Rodgers, dear friend, designer of *Mark the Music* and of Dryad Press books.

Prefatory Note

This note is to explain why I have included Hebrew and Yiddish translations. I felt warmed when Herman Taube first translated a number of these poems into Yiddish and Moshe Dor several into Hebrew. Though I speak neither language, I grew up with the sounds and cadences of both: Yiddish in the home, the "other" language of an immigrant family that withheld its fluency from children who were to be thoroughly Americanized; Hebrew in the synagogue where I learned the liturgies so well I can chant many of them today without the text. I have imagined that had I been a native speaker of Yiddish, Yiddish would have been the language of poems such as "Intercourse" and "Rejoice"; I feel the same about the Hebrew of "A Brief History" and "Take Hold." Back-to-back as they are, there is an invisible spine between them, though at the same time they point in different directions. As for Sabine Pascarelli's German translation of "Breakfast" — "Frühstück" — I can imagine my bilingual German-American granddaughters happening on this book sometime in the future and in leafing through it, reading the poem in English and in German and delighting in the gusto of both.

I

What I Want of It

I want it to graze like gazelles and soar with the aplomb of hawks.

I want it to rise like a palace out of syllables of breath.

I want it to open locked gates with obscure incantations.

I want it to kick down locked doors and lead into meadows of starlight.

I want it to light up the night with meteors of radiance and desire.

I want it to inflame the coldness of my heart and set passion on fire.

I want it to waken the mountain gods and startle the dead from boredom.

I want it to revive my ancestors and ask for their blessings.

I want it to guide me through deserts year after year and lead me to water and wild fruit.

I want it to open my eyes and reveal angels ascending and descending in my own backyard.

Metaphor

When metaphor speaks, she can say anything.
She is yellow dressing up as a socialite
or whore. She is your hair a soft avalanche of rain,
or light undressing herself and rising on fiery impulses of red.
She is your tongue like a humming bird or your palms
lifting sound from its sleep or storms raising
their hands in truce. Metaphor is in love with anything.
With small hills recalling mountains of memory.
Here she is, now, escorting you to the dinner
you were not invited to. She smiles as if you were the one love
of her life. The room glows with applause.
Metaphor is at your service — always, she says
and then adds, *just don't take me for granted. I am no
sentimental blonde. I have an accountant.
I pay my bills on time.* Metaphor knows her needs
and yours — and she charges accordingly. *Nothing is free*
she says and means it. When you have become too comfortable
metaphor will knock on your door bearing cut flowers
as though to say, *beautiful like us, yes, but how long can they last?*
Metaphor will walk into your house
as if she were your double. She will begin
mourning death in the most elaborate tropes —
she will speak of delicious grief, the sweet pain of sorrow,
the parting of love like rivers, all the lights in your father's house
are off forever. Metaphor lacks propriety.
Nothing is too much for her, or too little — she is insatiable,
forgets civility, rises in passionate anger. Just when you take her
for a friend, confessing everything, baring your nakedness
metaphor grabs hold of you like a mad cop and roughs you up.
Why, you ask? *For the hell of it*, she replies.
Count on nothing, she says, and throws you out into the dark.
Find your own way home, she calls. *I may be the arm on your shoulder.
Or the flood in your heart. Or the absence you back into.*

Stories

The sun has hardly sent its light over
the horizon and they are at your door clamoring,
rousting you from a deep sleep. Open at your peril.
A riot could break out like men crazy
for what you've got and they'll take it
if they want — listen to them battering the air.
                                    I am your birth story
one cries. I am your abandonment story cries another.
I am your adoption story shouts yet another wringing
its hands. I am the story of your youth shouts one.
And I the story of your dead parents, cries another.
I am your war story, the one you ran away from, another
shouts, though it is muffled by the lust story that is out there
raising hell. Up front, before me, weeping, is the marriage
story and the story of your children's departures.
Next to them, the nostalgia story is swooning in despair.
Beyond, dirtying the street are the stories of regret and revenge.
And near them, milling around, calling loudly, Listen, Listen
are the betrayal stories and the failure stories,
each desperate for attention. Whispering in torment
is the impotence story, and beside it the dementia story —
there too the stories of your cancer and the shrinking of the body.
Over at the side, huddled in a corner laughing hysterically
is the story of your former teeth and all those other
stories I've neglected, that I never had time for.
What a pandemonium of longing and rage.
                                    But beyond them all
at the far edge of the crowd is another I can hardly make out
at first. Silent, brooding, pushing its way ahead slowly. Slowly.
It is the story that every other has been whispering of for years,
the one not spoken of aloud that strikes fear and now, here,
suddenly, stills all their wild clamoring.

The Man Who Stole Laughter

*The poet has not a personality to express
but a particular medium, in which
imprecisions and experiences combine
in peculiar and unexpected ways.*
                              — *T.S. Eliot*

We were sleeping when he entered
The house was still as death
As he gathered up the laughter
That disappeared like breath.

The moon was shining fully
Against the stardrift night.
His face was red with fire —
His eyes stunned by light.

I felt his presence at my door
And never can forget
The silence that his body spoke
Of sorrow's sad regret.

I wanted to call out to him —
But was frozen in my bed.
He lingered there as though in need
Then turned away instead.

Before he disappeared I glimpsed
His eyes now dark and wild
And gave all hope to grief that night
And knew I was his child.

The Storied Past

*If you shine strong light on one side of
a problem, it casts long shadows on the
other. . . . One has to circle around the
problem again and again to illuminate all
the misconceptions that hold it in place.*
— *Ludwig Wittgenstein*

One story says I knew you
as a child. You were beautiful,
happy all the time, always smiling.
At four you made a story of the sun's rise
how it came out to play — sometimes
the sun felt sad, you said, unhappy
over the dark clouds that suddenly
would appear and keep it from playing.

Another story says I remember you
as a sad child, hesitant, unable to look anyone
in the eye. When you were four, your father,
for some reason I no longer remember
or never knew, went into a rage.
Trees came crashing down, a storm rose
rapidly in the living room. You crawled
terrified under the bed crying crying.
I wanted to do something but was helpless.

Isn't this strange to hear, says yet another story.
I remember us gathered all together.
You were performing like a prince
of the realm, your father all smiles of approval
and from your mother — ah! your mother she
held you in the gravitational pull of her heart.

Memory

You can stare at it in awe,
you can scrape the dirt from under
its nails, style it with accoutrements
or frame it like a photo. You can introduce it
at parties or hang it like a de Kooning
or Rothko on your living room walls.
You can massage its origins as well
with your therapist or sing O Sole Mio
in the shower each morning.

If your interests are novelistic
you may want to juggle its lack of plot
or rearrange its chronology for a
dramatic climax, all (of course)
in pursuit of Truth — O! Truth —
that holds us all in thrall.
If a poet, you might dress it
in stanza and rhyme or (more likely)
let the lines run free
in order to find themselves.
If a philosopher, you may analyze it
as a subjective category beset by linguistic
discontinuities and such.

Whatever you do, be cautious:
it could pitch you into a minefield
of metaphor where you may founder like a ship
listing in storm-toss'd ambiguities,
where there are no maps to guide you home.

If I do not remember thee, let my tongue cleave to the roof of my mouth. Psalm 137 ¶ From the table of my memory / I'll wipe away all trivial fond records, / All saws of books, all forms, all pressures past, / That youth and observation copied there. Shakespeare, Hamlet ¶ Memory is a strange Bell — Jubilee and Knell. Emily Dickinson ¶ To flee from memory / Had we the Wings. Emily Dickinson ¶ Along the brittle treacherous bright streets / of memory comes my heart.../ whispering like a drunken man / who (at a certain corner, suddenly) meets / the tall policeman of my mind. e.e. cummings ¶ April is the cruelest month, breeding / Lilacs out of the dead land, mixing / Memory and desire, stirring / Dull roots with spring rain. T.S. Eliot ¶ Why drag about this corpse of your memory, lest you contradict somewhat you have stated in this or that public place? Ralph Waldo Emerson ¶ Memory is a net; one finds it full of fish when he takes it from the brook; but a dozen miles of water have run through it without sticking. Oliver Wendell Holmes ¶ She unwound her ball of memories. Virginia Woolf ¶ Not the power to remember, but its very opposite, the power to forget, is a necessary condition for our existence. Sholem Asch ¶ Memory believes before knowing remembers. Believes longer than recollects, longer than knowing even wonders. William Faulkner ¶ Every man's memory is his private literature. Aldous Huxley ¶ My memory, my prison. Theodore Roethke ¶

Most [of what I remember] is probably filtered through the blown circuits of confusion and madness and is, I suppose, artful forgery, rigged document, a knocked-off passport of the soul. Stanley Elkin ¶ Looking back into memory ... is a great deal of invention, seeing yourself as others see you. Memory is the medium of must-have-been. Julian Jaynes ¶ His memory opened its gallery of waxworks, and he knew, he knew that there at its far end somewhere a chamber of horrors awaited him. Vladimir Nabokov ¶ We know how anecdotes are removed from storage like old clothes, spotted, brushed, and pressed, let out or taken in, and we carefully lace the sleeve of our personal history with lies, which really are revisions until eventually a formula for the past is settled on which (flattering or not) somehow suits us by concealing our nature. William Gass ¶ Everybody needs his memories. They keep the wolf of insignificance from the door. Saul Bellow ¶ Writers rearrange the world to suit their own views and needs. A.S. Byatt ¶ I don't solve the puzzle that the mesostic string presents. Instead I write or find a source text which is then used as an oracle. I ask it what word shall I use for this letter and what one for the next, etc. This frees me from memory, taste, likes, and dislikes. John Cage ¶ I think we will be able to alter memories someday to reduce the trauma from our brains. David Glanzman, neuroscientist ¶ I don't like to look back — I don't ask "what if." I look forward. Willie Mays

Our Block: A Play in One Act

Don't give us poems of unspeakable lives
If you can't make the words bleed.
— Madame Red

Missus Green
Old Missus Green
grinning
out her third floor window cried
sharply don't speak to me
of maybes or might have beens —
speak to me of lovers
running naked through fire —
my memory is alive with desire.

Stewed, pitiful,
in her cups, they all agreed,
Blue, that is, and Mrs. Orange
living next door and prim
Miss Yellow on the second floor
And Mr. Brown who merely nodded
on the park bench that fall
when the leaves were coloring
yet again and the warm winds lifted
them aloft while young mothers rolled
strollers past him. Mr. Brown invisible now
once had ladies in his thrall
or so he thought.

All of you are living lies
screamed Old Missus Green
from her third-floor window up there
to no one anywhere.

Poor old fracture, down for
the count, they nodded, drinking tea
and eating oatmeal cookies
passed out by Mr. Gray the Super
that last afternoon
of Old Missus Green on our block.

Mrs. Brown

Mrs. Brown's gone down.
Underground. Dead.
They all gathered once more
at Mrs. B's door.
Mrs. Orange wanted to cry
and though she tried, the best she could do
was a longish sigh. Miss Yellow could not speak.
Her heart, she said, was much too weak.
I'll have no part in this, said Madame Red
from her bed on the second floor.

Don't mourn for me
Mrs. Brown once said when she was feeling
grim — and once again when she
was feeling light and free. When you're dead
you're dead — life's justa show:
stagehand or star, over and over again
it's the same old play.
Mr. Brown sat in the park until dark that day and fed
bread crumbs to the birds. I'm all words
he muttered to himself, words and more words.

Mrs. Orange

I was pretty once
Mrs. Orange wept.
Great gams, Mr. O once said
so long ago when we were fresh
and I was new.
My chin's gone now, my cheeks sag.
Oh what's the use she said
over hot tea one bright afternoon.
Everything creaks
Mr. O's gone — good riddance.

I should have sinned more.
That time behind the kitchen door
when Blue grabbed at my waist
and bent down to kiss my breast

I was wet inside and could have cried
for the pleasure of it all.
And Mr. Brown once gave me sweets
and things, came pleading that we
go to bed. Look at him feeding pigeons
in the park — he might as well be dead.

You shoulda sinned, they all joined in.
You shoulda sinned.
You shoulda sinned.

Mr. Black

Ah dohn know whut we wan uv life
Ids filld with grace an filled wid strife —
When mah wife left mah light wen out
And what's left uv it.

Ah seen more than ah need tuh see
There's no 'un — nuthin — left fuh me.
Mah wife's dead, mah kids gone bad
Ah coulda been driven mad.

But here ahm at, ahv done nothin wrong
And ahm nowhir that ah belong.
On the streets, ahm yestiday's news
Some say that's just Black singin his blues.

Mr. Blue's Song

Bomb the bastards
Bomb the bastards
Bomb the bastards
Bomb

Bomb the bastards
Bomb the bastards
Bomb the bastards
Bomb

Miss Yellow

Miss Yellow, sickly, sweet
prim, proper, pinched, looks down a lot.
Lived with momma 40 years who up
and left Miss Y behind. She's weak of heart
she says and has a small role on the block,
says Mr. Gray. Double-locked behind her door
she sings in the choir in her mind
and sends her prayers aloft each night
but never screams like Missus Green
or cries like Mrs. O
or mocks life like Mrs. Brown
once did. She never says I should have
nor should not have. See Miss Yellow sit.
Long ago she loved a boy but has no memory of it.

Mrs. Blue

Mrs. Blue worked hard and did
all that she'd been taught to do.
Cleaned the house, made the beds,
cooked the meals, raised the kids.
Her rooms were spotless, no mess for her
but Mr. B was never there
even when he was.
And that's the sad short tale of Mrs. Blue
All the tenants cry boo hoo, boo hoo.

Madame Red

Madame Red receives visitors
in her bedroom and special
visitants in her bed. I can view the days
ahead she says and what the future
holds for you and you and you.
For Blue, and poor Miss Yellow
and Mrs. O on the floor below.
I once was with Mr. O, it was no good.
Nor Mr. Brown, soft as he was in both heads.

And Blue was all beery talk.
But that's been long ago and gone.
We're all done friends, all done.
That's the future that I see and what I see
is what I see.

Mr. Gray

I seen it all, says Mr. Gray the Super.
Yeah I seen it all even what I ain't
and I seen plenty. Mr. Brown for one —
he collected rents and was a good time man
until he went dry with Mrs. B,
when he was forty, then turned soft like putty.
How do I know what I know? Maybe I'm like
Madame Red who sees the future
from her bed and takes one man in after
another there, like Mr. O once and even Blue
who didn't know what to do. He liked his beer,
and kept his missus in her place who walked in fear
of him. And Mrs. O — she was a looker
once and wanted more than she ever got.
She's not right up there, something's dim —
it wasn't always so. Oh it's grim all right, grim.
Miss Yellow double-locked behind her door
and Missus G, she was a howler night and day,
day and night. And Black, he's suffered
more than most. There's more, of course, but we all know
the score. That's all, said Mr. Gray the Super.
That's all there is to say.

M's Coda

This is the end of our small play.
Let's away away as in Shakespeare's day —
We'll find new players and another stage
To strut and storm and laugh and rage.

Improvisations

1.
Old agers holding each others' hands
Their mouths in a settled frown —
Are they propping each other up
Or dragging each other down?

2.
Once in a tall tree
I grew wings and rose high
high into the sky and flew
like a blue sword through the night.
I descended into the day
Slicing off the heads of stems.

3.
She sinks the teeth of her despair
so deep into my heart
I am bleeding to death.

4.
An escaped word
lifts itself at a window
looking for a place to rest
if only for a moment.
I have seen it hunted down
tortured and taken out
for public confession.

April Inventory

That death has arrived here
there is no obvious sign — the mirrors
are not covered nor are there
hard benches to remind you
this is a house in mourning. The rooms
have been taken over by the steamy
yellow of cut forsythia brightening
the early light that sails in like the scent
of honey through these large windows.
For a man who scorned belief
of a world beyond, he has acted Pharaonic
having demanded that all his photographs,
his Mencken and Benchley, and all his stories
accompany him below.
                              Who are you?
I never asked. May I enter? Can we speak?
His children together now remembering
a memory here and another and another
which rise involuntarily — and they keep rising
as though they needed something to hold onto.
It knows no explanation, this grabbing hold of,
this inexplicable wanting, of which we are all
intimate and will go to our own deaths with
— that solitary desire he wrote
secretly to a younger woman in his old age,
Somewhere I have been searching
Out in the void of nothingness the unattainable —
Come with me behind the black curtain that is my life.

Heart of Darkness

Here, take this as you will.
Warning or caution — an offering.

Darkness is falling in his heart.
If you found your way in
you might descend deep into its ravines
you might get caught in its thickets
and lose all sense of direction.
You might wander for days and burn up
with fever. Thirst would ravage you.
You might be blinded by heat
and die of abandonment.
Listen — I know the heart
is a metaphor for the body's
need and the soul's hunger. Mine
is omnivorous. It knows no limits.
And yours?

Morning Takes

I will serve up nothing for M this morning
says Memory: you're on your own, pal —
find your poem somewhere else today
I'm tired of serving up tales
as though I were a machine
for grinding out epiphanies.
Go! Reach beyond the borders
of recall. Listen to the birds
pitching their cheeps
into the morning air
and scooting about like sex-crazed rascals.
Make something of them
why don't you.
Leave me alone.
Let the past lay fallow
for seven years (at least).

⁓

X calls distraught. Her husband Y
has been fucking Z for years
and she's just found out.
Ten fucking years M, says X. Incredulity.
Amazement. Wonder. My enemy
X says in disbelief.
When did they? Where?
And how could he get it up
for her?
　　　　Grief. Anger. Derision.
The dark side of living, says M
to himself, the eternal themes:
Infidelity and Despair.
How did I get here, cries X? Who am I?
What am I to do? Her sentences scoot
from one perch to the next,
then are off again like an erratic breeze.

How can you be shocked, asks M.
You haven't slept in the same bed
for years.

You are not coming in
Cries X, do you read me?
You are not coming in.

⁓

The sky through the leafing trees
back here has begun to brighten.
The squawks and cheeps are up and
pitching about from one branch
to the next, alighting, then aloft
and off again. Heigh Ho! they shout.
Meal Time. Let's get over to M's house —
a sweet bowl of sunflower seeds
sits on the sill.
            Yum.

The Lady and Her Shadow

The lady had thin
yellow hair. She
walked with a limp and could hardly
bear
the sun and so hid from
the man with balloons
who had
a wide toothy
masculine grin
and
were truth known
was one
of the demons
of air.
      Of fair
complexion he
a bit opaque, biceps
like brick, an engineer
counting
his data by two's
then by three's
divided
by the square root
of whatever
agrees.

And this
may sound silly
to you but it
wasn't at all
to the lady
with thin yellow hair
who died
of exposure
not from the sun
but the leer

of the man
with the wide toothy
grin and biceps
like brick
who walked on the beach
with balloons
in the air
and grinned at the lady
with yellowy hair
who
knew not enough
to get up
      and scoot away
                 quick like a fish
                     outta there.

Points of View

Fairy wrens mate for life, but are classic philanderers.
After doing his duty at home, the male visits every female
next in the vicinity. He frequently comes courting with
an offering of flowers in his beak.
                                          — *American Scientist*

His

Her story has no shame. It will reveal
everything whether you can bear it or not.
It will undress itself before you, it will remove
veil after veil, breathe softly into your ear.
It will give you sharp pointed bites everywhere
or preen like the bird of paradise.
It will appeal to your heart. It will do
anything for your devotion. It will barge
naked into your closed arms. Once started
it cannot stop. You're in for the long haul
unless you can tear away. You try to back away
but it comes after you pleadingly.
Tears spill from its words, words flood from its mouth.
sentences, now, entire paragraphs, page after page,
whole novels that pile up and block
your escape. Scream for help as you will
but no one can hear. What must I do to make you
listen, it pleads? Must I get on my hands and knees?
Must I open my heart with a knife and cover your feet in blood?

Hers

His story has no shame. It will tell you
nothing, while purporting to tell all.
It will tell you what you want to hear.
Come into my room it says, sit down, have some wine
or champagne. It will speak of architecture and architectonics.
It will speak grandly of purpose, of symbols, of myth
and poetry. It will go on endlessly about existentialism
and complexity theory. It will move to the difficulty

of love. Once started, it cannot stop. Its sentences
flow endlessly, they unfold one after another
like new wings and are soon off and soaring
on warms drafts of rhetoric far into the empyrean.
It smiles with self-satisfaction. And I sit there
staring in disbelief. Is this some joke? This is not
your story I say. It averts its eyes, grows uncomfortable.
Its anger rises and begins to storm. The wings have closed in.
It is all strut now, then rage. It is slamming doors, kicking in walls.
Expect nothing, I say, and you get nothing. Expect everything
and you get nothing still. It sits slumped over,
withered. It is tired, it says, it is tired of talking.
Yes I cry out, my words on fire,
tired of my truths as I am tired of your lies.

Opera Americana

Dear M
I'm so glad we found one another.
Rather that I found you, in your book.
What a surprise! I've been writing one too
About the family — some of whom you knew.

The Hatfields
           Brother G__ married a girl
named D__. They could not have kids — both died
four years ago. Brother B___, the youngest,
married twice, and had six by the two —
he lived in VT and died early at forty.
My sister J___ married a guy named L__
and had four kids — she was a smoker (and how),
got lung cancer and died in MO three years ago.
I married S and stayed so for sixty years —
we lived on a farm in MD, raised cattle,
retired and moved to NC. Ended back here
in a home. S__ lived six months
and died three years ago. We had one son,
ex-Navy, a nurse — a pilot as well.
He was trimming trees when a branch broke
and landed on him — he left one daughter
and two granddaughters, now 20 and 30.
I last heard they were living in MT.

The McCoys
           J__ died last year.
He had married a gal from NY, then moved to UT.
She's dead too. M__ married twice: the first to F__.
They had four kids; then to N__ — they had none.
Both F and N are gone. Where the children are I don't
know.
C__ lost his wife quite a few years ago
and is now in a nursing home in OK.
The B__ brothers all scattered, the three of them.
All gone, as far as I know.

It seems I have only written of death.
At our age, what else is to be expected. I read
all of your poems and enjoyed them much. (You too
write of death.) I gave them to a friend
who also writes poems — she had not heard of you.
What a poet, she said when she did. And how! I said.

That's it for now. What fun to find an old friend.
We used to have so much fun with all of our friends
back then. Do you remember?

Montaigne & Me

That to Philosophize Is to Learn to Die.

When you are young death is a skyscraper and only as you grow and time falls away like skin does it reveal itself to be an old world tailor, so fastidious, so precise.

~

Death's boatman takes no bribes

Death is the mother and father of Progress. Death may be money in your pocket. Death will keep after you as if to remind you the rent is due.

~

How is it possible that we should disengage ourselves from the thought of death or avoid fancying that it has us every moment by the throat?

Death is a sweet pickle for poets and a pork barrel for morticians.

~

Death's a great disguiser.

Underneath your eyelids the canopy is all in white, death's long fingers are waving like flags in a May breeze. Bodies press together to make benedictions. Death applauds giddily like a child.

~

I have made it my custom to have death not only in my imagination, but continually in my mouth.

The e in death is a tenor vowel: pronounce its name fully and with proper attention to texture: do you feel your teeth cut into the soft plane of your tongue? Now, roll the tip of your tongue onto the backside of your teeth and up into the roof of your mouth. Suck into your throat. Swallow.

Farewell

In these faces it is always farewell.
You may see yourself here or not.
You may walk a straight line to hell
And arrive through the front door or knock

Without thinking at the back.
You may be schooled in caution like a spy
And count every step and still backtrack
Into the arms of the enemy.

You may crawl on your knees for a hundred years
And engrave a yellow star on your breast.
You may try and cover your fears
And pretend you have come to a rest.

Dear friends, we are traveling this way
Alone. Finally, there are no lies.
Minute by minute, day by day,
Each life is a blessing, each blessing a disguise.

Interlude

A Short History

היסטוריה קצרה

Listen —
do you hear the music
in the earth that
makes us run? Of
birth and death
and in between the little
violences lifting their
scarred hands
in one poor truce after another?

הַקְשִׁיבוּ—
הֲתִשְׁמְעוּ אֶת הַמּוּסִיקָה
בְּנִבְכֵי הָאֲדָמָה
שֶׁמְּרִיצָה אוֹתָנוּ? עַל
אוֹדוֹת לֵידָה וּמִיתָה
וּמַה שֶּׁבֵּין מַעֲשֵׂי הָאַלִּימוּת
הַקְּטַנִּים הַמְּרִימִים אֶת
יְדֵיהֶם הַמְּצֻלָּקוֹת
בִּשְׁבִיתוֹת-נֶשֶׁק עֲלוּבוֹת הַחוֹזְרוֹת וְנִשְׁנוֹת

THE NATION'S GUN SHOW

BUY • SELL • TRADE

APRIL 15, 16 & 17
Fri. 3-8 • Sat. 9-5 • Sun. 10-5

DULLES EXPO CENTER
CHANTILLY, VA
Largest Gun Show in Metro DC!

1000 TABLES! The size of 2 football fields! Over 1.5 miles of
Guns, Knives and Accessories!

GET YOUR GUNS WHILE YOU STILL CAN!!!

NRA National Firearms Museum presents "The Golden Guns" Five of the
most elaborately embellished firearms in the world, with almost more gold
than steel. These fine arms are from the Robert E. Petersen Gallery.

JOIN OR RENEW YOUR NRA MEMBERSHIP AND GET IN FREE.

All firearm sales subject to local, state and federal law.
Modern and Antique Firearms • Ammo • Knives • Coins • Books & more!

  Showmasters inc.

WP

★ www.TheNationsGunShow.com • 1-888-715-0606 ★

April 12, 2011

Sniper

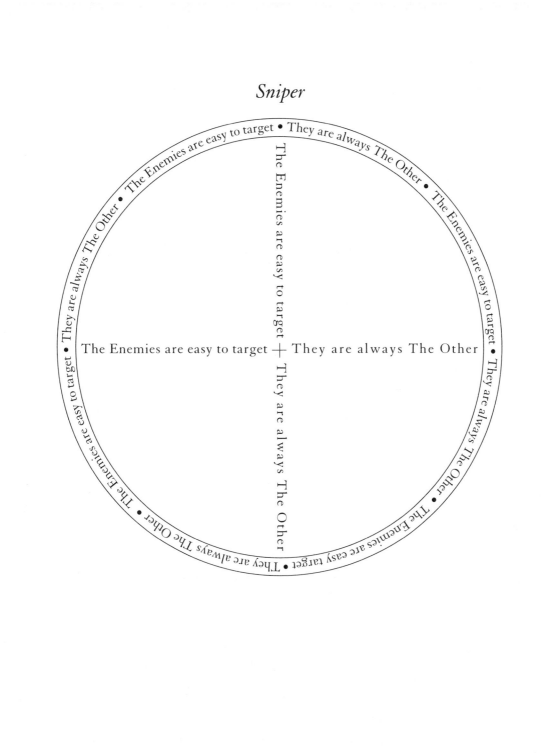

Witness

For the crime of killing a man the state
of Florida today killed John Arthur
Spenkelink. At 10:12 a.m., the first
of three surges of hundreds of volts raced
through his slight body, ending his life of
thirty years. So snugly was he strapped and
restrained in an old oaken electric
chair that he barely moved.
                                                    Before an
electrician lowered a veil over
his face, his eyes were filled with hopeless terror,
some of the official witnesses said.
He wore dark blue prison pants and a white
shirt rolled up at the sleeves. His head was shaved.
Thirty-two witnesses seated in an
adjoining room, their vision of the
electric chair blocked by a blind, heard a door
clang shut. Then at 10:11 a.m.
abruptly and without warning, the blind
was raised. There he sat: his pants were rolled up
to the knees. An electrode was attached
to his shaved right calf and both legs strapped.
Wide leather straps bound his waist chest arms and
wrists. A white towel tied around his neck
kept his head up and back, and a thick black
strap covered his mouth. His eyes were wide open,
almost bulging and he looked straight ahead
at the witnesses including two standing
in the back of the room, the two men who
had fought for his body and his soul —
his lawyer and his minister.

Reaching
over to the skullcap that bore a metal
knob on top an electrician with heavy
gloves lowered over his face the black flap
that would bar to all Spenkelink's last look

44

at life. They had seen his gaze for thirty
seconds or so. At 10:12 a.m. a
noise and the first burst of electricity
hit him. His chest heaved, his right fist clenched
and his left hand moved. The legs jerked. The flesh
on his right leg seared, by one account, and smoke
rose into the death chamber. A few inches
below the electrode cuff on his calf,
there was a three-inch wound. It looked as if
his skin had split, but there was no blood.
The smell of burning blood did not reach the
official witnesses. His hands turned blue,
especially near the fingertips.

Two minutes later, a doctor checked
Spenkelink's heart beat with a stethoscope
unbuttoning his white shirt and raising
his undershirt.
            The doctor stepped back and
a second bolt hit Spenkelink. The doctor
repeated his exam and stepped back again.
A third surge of electricity was
started but was ended before its full
cycle. And at 10:18 a.m. the doctor
checked for a pulse and a heart beat
and peered into Spenkelink's eyes with a
penlight.
            It was very antiseptic
one witness said, very professional
said another. It was respectful of
a man's privacy in the moment of his public death.

Adapted from Bill Curry,
The Washington Post, *May 26, 1979*

Lament

They
They are
They are waiting
They are waiting to
They are waiting to accuse
They are waiting to accuse you
They are waiting to accuse you and
They are waiting to accuse you and do
They are waiting to accuse you and do away
They are waiting to accuse you and do away with
They are waiting to accuse you and do away with you
They are waiting to accuse you and do away with
They are waiting to accuse you and do away   They
They are waiting to accuse you and do   They are
They are waiting to accuse you and   They are waiting
They are waiting to accuse you   They are waiting to
They are waiting to accuse   They are waiting to accuse
They are waiting to   They are waiting to accuse you
They are waiting   They are waiting to accuse you and
They are   They are waiting to accuse you and do
They   They are waiting to accuse you and do away
They are waiting to accuse you and do away with
They are waiting to accuse you and do away with you
They are waiting to accuse you and do away with
They   They are waiting to accuse you and do away
They are   They are waiting to accuse you and do
They are waiting   They are waiting to accuse you and
They are waiting to   They are waiting to accuse you
They are waiting to accuse   They are waiting to accuse
They are waiting to accuse you   They are waiting to
They are waiting to accuse you and   They are waiting
They are waiting to accuse you and do   They are
They are waiting to accuse you and do away   They
They are waiting to accuse you and do away with
They are waiting to accuse you and do away with you
They are waiting to accuse you and do away with
They are waiting to accuse you and do away
They are waiting to accuse you and do
They are waiting to accuse you and
They are waiting to accuse you
They are waiting to accuse
They are waiting to
They are waiting
They are
They

Negotiation

This is mine
And this
And this right here.
You can have that
And that —
And that over there.

But I want this
And this
And this right here.

I said
You can have that
And that —
And that over there.

But I must have this
And this
And this right here.
It is mine.
It has always been.

Was.

You are choking me
Without this
And this
And this right here.

Tuscarora War, 1711

Yamasee War, 1715-18

Pontiac's Conspiracy, 1763

Lord Dunmore's War, 1774

Northwest Indian War, 1785-95

Battle of Tippecanoe, 1811

Creek War, 1813-14

First Seminole War, 1816-42

Second Seminole War, 1835-42

Navajo Conflicts, 1846-63

Sioux Wars, 1854-90

Rogue River War, 1855-56

Apache Attacks, 1861-1900

Ute Wars, 1865-68; 1879

Battle of the Rosebud, 1876

Modoc War, 1872-73

Red River War, 1874-75

Battle of the Little Big
Horn/Battle of the Greasy
Grass, 1876

Nez Percé War, 1877

Wounded Knee Massacre, 1890

Choke then.

It was my father's,
My father's father
And his father's, and his . . .

You can have that
And that —
And that over there.

I cannot breathe.
You cannot do this.
I will die.

You can have that
And that —
And that over there.

Fuck you
And your children
And your children's children.
You cannot do this.

And you
And your children
And your children's children.

FOUR POEMS BY EYTAN EYTAN

Translated from the Hebrew by Merrill Leffler and Moshe Dor

Around

On the left you will find the blood-stained dew
And on the right you will find the blood-stained dew

One day the wet grass
And one day the dry grass

A sacrifice of killed flesh
Always the slaughtered flesh

Go on go on speak poetry to them

The Rain Is Ready to Fall

The rain is ready to fall
On the mountains of the deep
On the high valleys.
The rain is ready to fall downside up
On the defeated victors
On the victorious defeated.
The rain is ready to fall on a world turning upside down.
A rain of many waters.
A rain the earth can only accept.

Children/Yeladim

Children/yeladim you who will die in the next war
Burnt up in tanks or ripped by splintered shells, shocked
Your hands and your limbs torn from you
Be not afraid
Be not afraid of its arrival
Because you will die in the next war
Suddenly or slowly or with no warning or during a desperate fight
Be not afraid now and fear not its arrival
Because death will take you in war and without war
At its own choosing

Children/yeladim you are and you will die in the next war
Following a deafening furor
Because there is no war without death and no war without furor
And no life without death at its own choosing

Rush not to swallow the poison awaiting you
And rush not to love or to hate
Hold no hope for rescue or that war will not come
Because it will
And battle awaits you
Torn flesh burnt bodies and spilled blood and gray shriveled bones
And hovering ghosts

Yeladim you who will die in the next war
Will leave this valley of tears with nothing
The righteous will continue to cheat and to steal and to send you into the next war
  to die under a bright sun or a dark moon or the remote stars
Beneath you will lie in the shivering earth

Because you will die yeladim
And cannot escape from death
You will fear no more when in your deaths
While those who remain will weep they will weep for themselves
And your souls will tremble in transparence and light
Over this accursed earth where flesh covers bone
And over this accursed earth where man has forever chased after war

There are no grounds for fear. Yeladim you are
And children you will die. No brothers to you are your enemies and your brothers
   are your enemies.
Because a gun has an aim when it speaks
It is better that the warrior die than be butchered in retreat

I am speaking of my contempt for death
Of my contempt for the death you will die in the next war
I speak plainly and I speak truth

Fires will burn through the night, fires
Ships will sink in the sea, ships
Men will fall in the dark, men

Phone lines will be severed, power
Bridges will give way, roads
Transmitters will be shattered
Journalists bodies impaled, writers
Cars will burn and the thick stench of corpses
Will burn your eyes, your throats

You from the hills of Ephraim, from the hills of Judea
You from the coastal plain, you from the ruins of Jerusalem.
You who hold each others' hands and you who grasp another's heels none
   will survive you

I am speaking to you
I am speaking from the valley of death
I am speaking from the valley of death that will rise in a mound of corpses

Poisoned the reservoirs and the air poisoned
The people will seek shelter and the children will howl
The old, the women will cry out with death in their mouths

No blood will be spilled
Why spill blood
Why kill in blood

A dove will awaken in smoke
Its voice in song
Its smoke-filled voice alone, its smoke-drenched wings beating alone

A voice from the valley of death
A troupe passes in silence
Turmoil breaks loose from its cage

Rubble, ashes, bones, mountains of plastic and rusted cans
The dead cannot scratch
Nor can the living

But why
Can someone say why
What says the speaker
Or even the righteous
A bald one and she-bears
None have survived, ascend ascend
With one stone, take my mantle
A chariot of fire of fire in the sky
To the sea runs a stream of blood
Take my mantle, let the stream stop
Let earth bring forth manure and milk and fruit and meat
Let the earth split open and swallow half the people

On the highway east of Jordan an orphan of purple light stands on the ridged hills
The winds scream through the body, relent, then begin again
My cold body flat against the earth a part of the earth apart from the earth
  the winds battering the earth

The moon spreads its cold light over the mountain.
Elohim's chill bitter cold, lonely. A face standing.
How full the soul is, how full the souls float over moonlight fills the mountain,
  hovering over the mountain full of light, the light-filled souls

I was a child standing in death
Dissolving in the mists sinking and dissolving
On the hard earth my feet stepped through mists

I have felt nourished in a gray field of blood nourished have I felt
I've seen a child and have been nourished
I was a child in a gray field of blood I was

Fully alive
A shadow falls along the River Jordan
Taking sharp turns

From the mountains a shadow falls
Rising from the valley
Shivering in a dense wet fog

The shadow of a dove, a tree heavy with sleep
A tree heavy with sleep in the mountains
The shadow is fire, a body trapped in darkness

Patches of light and thunder
What of the body's trembling in sickening explosions
Bodies touch, cling in the shivering earth

It's shivering, silently shivering, pleading, come to me
In the end come to me come into the sea in the light of day come in the hot sun
    beneath a hot sun come to me again
In my trembling come on me. Come in my trembling

And comes the singing of angels coming white in the morning light
Light of morning the singing of angels
White singing of angels white as death in life

The Wind Grinds

The wind grinds bones to dust
In the courtyard of death
Grinds clouds, vehicles
In a low continuous burning
Grinds soldiers, grinds cannon and guns
Grinds buildings, grinds animals, grinds you and me

Listen, leave your explosives, your vehicles, your soldiers
Leave your animals, your wars, your people
They all left you long ago

You have the wind with you
You have the burning light, the land and the dew with you
You have the whole pulverized earth with you

Set your face towards begetting
Set your face once more toward rising

II

The Maw of Art

I saw the opening maw of hell.
                          — Herman Melville

The maw of art feeds
                                and feeds
                                                and feeds
Insatiable
                the sun's fiery setting
                                                black night
you name it
                horned owl
                                vulture
                                                crows
on a winter branch
                                where late the sweet birds
                                                                yes
on some balcony
                                Rockville Pike
                                                the Green Mountains
wherever you are
                                come see the maw of art
                                                                at work
on its knees
                before
                                the bloody afterbirth
                                                        an orphaned child
rivers rising
                relentlessly
                                the anonymous dead
these arias of earth
                                singeth the maw of art
                                                        they would
live
        and live
                in my ⌐ heart
                                forever⌐

Performance

Do you think the I standing before you
doesn't want to seduce your attention
and hold you close to the erratic beating
of its heart? Do you think the I here is not performing
for your applause and approbation,
that it's not needy or demanding
and doesn't want more than it knows it's entitled to,
that it won't pull from its hat every possible trick —
its brooding soulfulness, its comic shtick —
whatever it takes?
                    Friend, look in the mirror.
Show me we are not a marriage of grief and joy,
of lust, desire, ambition, fear, of every need
that has clung since we were first thrust into this dark
and resplendent world, that all our stunting
our juggling, our masks, all our art and philosophy
want nothing from each other and are not in performance.
Friend, mon frère, ma soeur, astonish us.

Struttin'

Cocka-Doodle-Do

You talk your puffed up walk
Cocka doodle heap
of struttin' stuff. Watch out (you say) —
in my way or out
I'll part the darkness
stridin' through her
like a Moses through the Sea —
I'm a high flyin' Outta My Way
Cocka the Walk Cat —
the winds at my feet
and the Chicks so sweet — no countin'
how many hangin' out and on.
O Masta' (they say)
you no ordinary mista' —
you in your prime
and we got the time

Chorus
Just wait, hot shot. The end
of days is not so long
and we'll be waiting
your final song.

≈

Roscoe of Takoma Park

Behold me here, imprisoned now in bronze
Where once I held command of this great street —
Cock of the Walk who strode with Rooster gods.

O Roscoe you're the One, just like the Fonz
Was once, they'd cry and bow down at my feet.
Behold me now, imprisoned here in bronze.

I strutted all about just like the Lords
My coxcomb high — I was more than great —
Cock of the Walk who strode with Rooster gods.

I had an eye for Chicks — and with my fowl glands
I took the measure of their tender meat.
And now? Look at me fettered here in bronze.

Oh! I'd rather be a lonely Hen who plods
Each day and has to beg the smallest treat.
Aieee, me, Roscoe who strode with Rooster gods.

So go you Passersby and Common Clods —
Know that you too will leave in damned defeat.
Gaze on at me now imprisoned here in bronze
Cock of the Walk who strode with Rooster gods.

Dismantling

Be willing to dismantle for the purpose
of rebuilding on more solid structure.
— *Horoscope*

First you must lift the idea
(be careful it may be heavy)
and haul it out to the dumpster.
Next locate the meaning — it may not
come easily, though if you have
the right tools and they are good tools
you should have no difficulty. Now
it is the sentences' turn: take each one
strip it of grammar (you may need
abrasives here) and hang them all
on a line. When thoroughly dried,
lay each one down on the grass or
if you live in the city, the sidewalk will do.
The point is, make sure you put them
in harm's way, wherever you are.
Don't try to protect them. It may be
they will go to war, or wander the desert
or haunt the streets like beggars
or run from the police or suffer
loneliness and despair. Remember:
they must make their own way. The best
you can do is to stay out of theirs
and take them back in if they return.

May(be)cause

you haven't heard from the sun in four days
or the days are on a stampede to nowhere
or all art is manipulative even the most saintly
or meaning itself is as remote as the sky
or if god is god he is not good
or if god is good he is not god (MacLeish)
or the chairs are collapsing under my weight
and the bills are making a constant racket
while the passing of beauty is too painful
or meanness seems to have its foot to the pedal
or poems want to somersault and do handstands
but have tired legs and crawl under the covers
or I cannot read all the books shouting at me
and those I've read I no longer remember
or I've become invisible and am late again with my taxes
or death and departure are closing in
or I am a bare breath in the earth's respiration
while melancholy rises like the tides and is drowning my mind
or the world is a charnal house and a brothel (I.B. Singer)
or there is no (may)be and no (be)cause

WPSY Streaming

Hello, this is Barbara, 28
Do you hear me? Hello?
Am I on?
I'm scared, I'm still trying though.
What can I do?

> *Of course you're scared. You have*
> *Shaky legs. The foundation rocks. Be calm.*

Î was wondering, that's all.

> *Wonder is good, Barbara.*
> *Just don't forget the strengths*
> *You've acquired in these years of therapy.*
> *Can you remember three things*
> *You've learned? Can you say them?*

I am what I am is one. My mistakes are no different
Than the President's or the Pope's is a second.
And a third is, take two valium,
One on rising and one in the dead of night.

> *Good for you Barbara.*
> *Just don't forget your inner light.*

Hello this is Dave, 26.
Hello, I am Chris. I am 27
I am in a potential extramarital affair.
I need help with the anxiety
I'm sure to encounter there.
Help me please — how can I prepare?

> *Walk into the anxiety itself, Chris*
> *And observe your heart. Massage it gently*
> *And wake up its feelings — feelings are all.*
> *Do you understand?*

Thank you doctor. Listen, I saw you
On the Morning Show and
You are quite attractive. Doctor
I wonder . . .

Good afternoon, you're next on WPSY

Hello, I am Theresa, aged 24.
I don't know what to do.
I am alone in the dark
And I am crying all the time.
I cannot keep the floods back.

I understand your grief, Theresa.
I have been in the dark myself
And can say, let your grief out
Into the light of day.

Hello, I am Allen, age 70.
I talk and talk but still have a communications
Problem. It has gone on for years.
She refuses to see her mistakes
When I point them out to her.

Do you love her Allen?
Do you cherish and honor her?
Is there enough foreplay? Or are you
Another selfish male intent only
On your own excited itch?

Hello, this is Margaret, age 45.
I want to be emotionally available
Hello, this is Robert, 22. Do you hear me?
Hello, this is Dick Age 54 and life is not
What I expected. Hello this is Jane age 54 and
My dog Spot died and I am suicidal. Hello.
Hello.

To the Failed Suicides

Finally you have returned.
You have walked back
Onto the narrows of your life.
Once more the shore has
Raised itself. Grasses root
Even in sand.
           This says nothing
About hope. What is dead remains dead —
And you have left something
Of your life behind.
           But you are back
From the spaces where there are no walls,
Where words are like rain
And hands have given up on gestures.

It is not that I claim privileged understanding.
If I have sat on more than one occasion
With my feet crossed and my fists
Tight like stone to keep the body
From crumbling, that is no special knowledge.

But I have seen you pass in poor parade,
The soldiers of loss. I am no herald.
I would not presume to speak of victory.
What I can speak of is the blood
Riving its way in all things forever
Rock, tree, weed, the fingers
Gripping tight to a rail overlooking
The city's panorama of lights,
Resisting the dread pull of the earth's center.

Failure

*Even the happiest man, the one most envied by
the world, in nine cases out of ten his inmost
consciousness is one of failure.*
                                        — *William James*

The rosy dawn slips underneath your sleep
and wakens you to failure sitting
on your bed. She whispers seductively.
Even before you've relieved your bladder
or brushed your teeth or walked out the door
for the paper, she crawls through your body
like a lover, her hands all over you.
She cannot get enough, she says. She believes in you,
speaks in a language you don't understand.
You don't need to, she says, leaning up against you
at work or staring back from the mirror —
it's the feeling that counts. I am with you
on your rising up and your lying down.
I am your companion — the wind whistling
through your sails, she croons, the rudder in your hand,
the sea in which you navigate. Think of me
she says as your sister separated from you at birth,
as your dark queen, your passionate other.
Failure welcomes you into her lavish rooms
or sits on a stoop in Baltimore, her arm around
your shoulder or on a subway rattling through Brooklyn,
or an arroyo in Mexico, or somewhere in the desert
where the heat has riven your body with drought.
She is the soul of generosity: ask nothing of her
and she will give all that she has —
ask for everything and she'll give that as well.
I call out the best in you, she sighs
like a lover. Come to me now —
if you could only love me the way I love you
we might even make poetry.

Limits

1.

Here says god the author of us all you are my
invention. What can I say, he says, I too am limited
in what I can create (*barah*). Once I had an idea
and worked like a poet driven mad by dreams, delighted
like every god before me. With such powers I imagined
a brave new world and took it on with gusto. What hubris!
After all, how much can I do? I also get writer's block.
I too get depressed. I too have limits
and am condemned to repeat myself. Meanwhile,
you bother me so with your petty woes. What about me?
I too could use compassion. Some pity on your part
wouldn't hurt. For god's sake, what would you be
without me, without even my dullest idea.
Enough already! I have given you the outline —
you make the plot. Go golem, travel as you will.
I wash my hands of you. You are no longer my business.

P.S. If you'd like, you can keep in touch.

*"Even God has problems . . .
I am not sure how we can help
Him."*
— Abraham Heschel

*"Man makes, God creates."
The Hebrew "barah" is used
exclusively for divine activity.
Man is spoken of as "making"
or "forming," but never "creat-
ing," i.e., producing something
out of nothing.*
— J.H. Hertz

2.

Here says god the author of us all you are my
invention. What can I say, he says, I too am limited
in what I can create (*barah*). Once I had an idea
and worked like a poet driven mad by dreams, delighted
like every god before me. With such powers I imagined
a brave new world and took it on with gusto. What hubris!
After all, how much can I do? I also get writer's block.
I too get depressed. I too have limits
and am condemned to repeat myself. Meanwhile,
you bother me so with your petty woes. What about me?
I too could use some compassion. Some pity on your part
wouldn't hurt. For god's sake, what would you be
without me, without even my dullest idea.
Enough already! I have given you the outline —
you make the plot. Go golem, travel as you will.
I wash my hands of you. You are no longer my business.

*"God is the only being who in
order to rule does not need
even to exist."*
— Baudelaire

ABRAHAM AVINU, OUR FATHER ABRAHAM
Three Poems from the Book of Genesis

Abraham and Hagar

And then you came to me that night at Beersheba.
Ah! Hagar slave that you were, given me by Sarah
Out of grief that for us there would be no son despite
His promise.
       And when you entered, wanting nothing more
I thought than to give me the son I so desired.
What did I know, what could I know of such fire
Married to Sarah my sister? In you I knew for the first time
The mercilessness of love — the heat of Egypt in your body.
You knew no shame. Each night you came to me,
Your veil covering such ruby lips.
       O! Hagar in you I learned
To unknow shame. You took my life in hand.
Of all my riches the richest was your nighttime body
And then our son. I love him for his sake.
I love him for yours. And I love him for mine.
Ishmael. Our son of passion.
       But then the Invisible One
Saw to it that Sarah's aged body bore me a second son.
Isaac. Her love of him grew with bitterness towards you.
What could I do when she screamed, *Drive out this slavegirl*
And her son (our son, Hagar) *for the slavegirl's son Ishmael*
Shall not inherit with my son, with Isaac.
I suffered her uncontrollable rage. No words
Could console her.
       Then Elohim came to me at night.
Whatever Sarah says, He said, *heed her voice, for through Isaac*
Shall your seed be continued. And through Ishmael, too,
I will make a nation, for he is your seed. My dearest Hagar
God had spoken — what could I answer?
He has provided for our son — I grieve my loss of you.
There is nothing more I can do.

Abraham and the Binding of Isaac

The final belief is to believe in a fiction, which you know to be a fiction, there is nothing else.
The exquisite truth is to know that it is a fiction, and that you believe in it willingly.
— *Wallace Stevens*

And so the story that is Genesis 22 begins: *And it happened after these things that God [Elohim] tested Abraham and said to him, "Abraham." And he said, "here I am."*

Here I am; in Hebrew *hineni*. "Such is the response of the pious," writes Rashi (1040-1105).

And He said: "Take, pray, your son, your only one, whom you love, Isaac, and go forth to the land of Moriah, and offer him up as a burnt offering on one of the mountains, which I will tell you of." (22:2)

Take, pray; in Hebrew *kach na*: an entreaty, an exhortation, not a summons, not an order — "nothing other than an expression of request," wrote Rashi. And Abraham's reply? Silence. Abraham who contended with God (Gen. 18:20-33) convinced Him to spare Sodom and Gomorrah if at least ten righteous men were living there: *"Far be it from You to do such a thing, to put to death the innocent with the guilty, making innocent and guilty the same. Far be it from you! Will not the Judge of all the earth do justice?"* (18:25) Was the poet himself so numbed by Abraham's silence that he could only write:

And Abraham rose early and saddled his donkey, and took two young servants with him and Isaac his son. (22:3)

Rashi: "He did not command one of his servants [as a man of his stature normally would] for love interrupts the correct order [of things.]"

And Abraham split the wood for the burnt-offering and went to the place that God told him of. On the third day Abraham raised his eyes and saw the place from afar. (22:4)

How distant was their journey? Did they rest on the way? What did they speak of? Did they cross the desert in silence?

And Abraham said to his servants, "Sit you here with the donkey and I and the lad will go yonder and we will worship and return to you." (22:5)

Abraham says, "we" will return — a foreshadowing? Was the poet following a script? Did he hold out hope that Elohim would relent, or Abraham, or himself?

And Abraham took the wood of the burnt-offering, and placed it on Isaac his son and took in his hand the fire and knife as the two of them went together. (22:6)

> Midrash Rabbah Genesis: "One to bind and the other to be bound, one to slaughter and the other to be slaughtered." And Rashi: "Abraham, who was aware that he was going to slaughter his son, was going with eagerness and joy, as Isaac, who was unaware of the matter." From Isaac we've heard nothing, until now.

"My father." And Abraham said, "Hineni, here I am, my son." And Isaac said, '"Here is the fire and the wood but where is the lamb for the offering?" (22:7)

> Can we discern grief in Abraham's, "my son"? Can we infer remorse or anguish? And did the poet believe that Father Abraham, Abraham Avinu, God contender, could slaughter his son on an altar of his own making? Many rabbis have rejoiced in Abraham's obedience to the Invisible One. Maimonides (1135-1204), for instance: "Abraham sought to kill Isaac because man's duty is to love and to fear God, even without hope of reward or fear of punishment." And would he, Maimonides, have done the same? Or Rashi: "Abraham, who was aware that he was going to slaughter his son was going with eagerness and joy — as Isaac, who was unaware of the matter."

And Abraham said: "God will see to the lamb for the offering, my son." So they went both of them together. (22:8)

> Was the poet stirred by the pathos of his story? Did he fear what he had to write? Was he torn between compassion for Isaac and Abraham's single-mindedness? Did he grieve for himself, for the duty he had to the story?

And they came to the place which God had told him of and Abraham built the altar there, laid the wood in order and bound Isaac his son, and laid him on the altar atop the wood. (22:9)

> And Isaac? Could he give himself up without struggling? According to some estimates, he was 37 years old, no lad like the servants awaiting his return. Solomon Ibn Gabirol (1021-1058), in the mind of Isaac: "Bind for me my hands and feet / Lest I be found wanting and profane the sacrifice. /I am afraid of panic, I am concerned to honor you, / My will is to honor you greatly." Is there any such son as the one Gabirol imagined?

And Abraham reached out his hand and took the knife to slaughter his son. (22:10)

How? How? The Knight of Infinite Resignation, wrote Kierkegaard (1813-1855): "I cannot think myself into the mind of Abraham . . . . Anyone who looks on this scene is paralyzed." But S. Yizhar (1916-2006): "I hate our father Abraham, who binds Isaac. What right does he have? Let him bind himself. I hate the God who sent him and closed all paths, leaving only that of the binding. I hate that Isaac serves as a mere test between Abraham and His God." But mirabilis!

And a messenger of the Lord YHWH called to him from heaven, and said: "Abraham, Abraham." And he said, "Hineni, here I am." (22:11) And he said: "Reach not your hand against the lad and do nothing to him, for now I know that you fear God and you have not held back your son, your only one, from Me." (22:12)

Had the author come to the edge of his own grief and at that last moment called up a deus ex machina? Not the poet Wilfrid Owen (1893-1918): "an angel called him out of heaven, / Saying, Lay not thy hand upon the lad, / Neither do anything to him. Behold, / A ram, caught in the thicket by its horns; / Offer the Ram of Pride instead of him. // But the old man would not so, but slew his son, / And half the seed of Europe, one by one."

And Abraham raised his eyes and saw a ram caught in a thicket by its horns and went and took the ram and offered him up for a burnt-offering instead of his son. And Abraham called the name of that place Adonai-yireh, as is said to this day, "On the mount of the Lord there is sight." (22:13-14)

Rashi on Abraham's dialogue with God: "You said to me, 'since through Isaac will offspring be considered yours.' And you subsequently said, '*Kach na*, take, pray your son.' Now you say to me, 'Do not send forth your hand at the lad.' The Holy One, Blessed is He, said to him, 'I will not profane My covenant and I will not deviate from that which has come forth from My lips. When I said to you, *kach na*,' . . . I did not say to you, Slaughter him, but rather, Bring him up.' You have brought him up. Take him down.'" An end to trauma? Haim Gouri (b.1923): "Isaac, as the story goes, was not sacrificed. / He lived many days more, / saw (life's) goodness, until his eyesight dimmed. // But he bequeathed that hour to his descendants. / They are born / with a knife in their hearts."

And the angel of the Lord called to Abraham a second time from the heavens (22:15)

> The Lord YHWH gave blessings, made promises to multiply Abraham's seed, as the stars in the heavens and as the sand on the shore of the sea, that they should possess the gates of the enemies, etcetera, etcetera (22:16-18)

So Abraham returned to his young servants and they rose up and went together to Beersheba (22:19)

> But where is Isaac? Was the poet so relieved in sending Abraham off to the next chapter, Gen. 23, that he forgot his promise to return Isaac to the servants? Was Isaac indeed sacrificed as some rabbis have written and later resurrected? Rabbi Ephraim ben Jacob of Bonn (1132-c.1175): "He made haste, he pinned him down with his knees, / He made his two arms strong. / With steady hands he slaughtered him according to the rite, / Full right was the slaughter. // Down upon him fell the resurrecting dew, and he revived. / (The father) seized him (then) to slaughter him once more. / Scripture, bear witness! Well-grounded is the fact: / And the Lord called Abraham, even a second time from heaven." Or did Abraham in fact fail his last trial by not contending with God, by not saying "I refuse. I am your servant but not your slave? And Sarah? Mother Sarah? Where was she in all these goings on?

Sarah

I knew and there was nothing I could do.
In matters of the One God I was no one —
No more to him than a mere presence, nothing.
The grief I felt welling up like a storm
I held back as though an ache
I had no right to possess.
Was I not the mother — did I not suffer
The birth? With him, God was no mystery.
Elohim, he said. Yahweh. El Shaddai. And
A hundred other names. That simple belief was more
Than I could contend with. I lacked power
Let alone will. My anger was like sand
Thrown against the desert winds.
I prayed to the Miraculous One
as if I believed there was purpose,
As if I believed the voice he said he knew
Like love in his heart. Fool, I cried,
You are the victim of a mad heart,
You are possessed by a demon that gives
Nothingness a name and then bows in submission.
He in his single-mindedness could no longer hear
But rose before dawn and took the son
Of my aged body, who himself obeyed
In ignorant trust, and journeyed for days
With a solemnity I would spit on.
When they returned I knew
Reasons would be given, explanations.
He, my husband who could raise
Words out of a sand storm as if that storm
Were guided, not by the former gods
Of our home but a viewless god who spoke
In syllables of air.

Two Midrashic Commentaries

When Abraham returned from Mt. Moriah, Samael [Satan] was angry when he saw that he had failed to stop Abraham's sacrifice. What did he do? He went and said to Sarah, "Oh Sarah! Have you not heard what has happened?" She said to him, "No." So he told her, "Your old husband took your son Isaac and brought him for a burnt-offering, and Isaac was crying and wailing that he could not be saved." Sarah immediately began to cry and wail. Three cries corresponding to three blasts from the shofar and three wails corresponding to three howls of the shofar. And her soul took flight and she died.

— Pirkei De-Rabbi Eliezer
(c. 100 C.E.)

When Isaac returned to be with his mother, she said to him, "Where have you been, my son?" He replied, "My father took me up mountains and down valleys, and took me up one of the mountains, built an altar, arranged the wood, prepared the offering-place, and took the knife to slaughter me, and an angel called out to him to stop. And Sarah said, "Woe unto my son! Were it not for the angel you would have already been slaughtered?" To which, Isaac answered, "Yes." They say that she died before finishing the six screams.

— Leviticus Rabbah, 20:2
(c. 5th-7th century)

Arise!

The poem is sleeping deeply in his body.
He calls lightly at first to awaken her
but she does not stir.

                He tries incantation
to break through the fog but she lies
dormant. He's driven to shake her
awake but she'll have none of that.
Sleep sweet sleep is what she wants.

Have pity for Christ's sake he shouts.
But nothing nothing.
He stalks about the room brooding
in hope she will waken
to his need. Nothing dark nothing.

Hear him now howling like a mad dog
howling howling to the blank fog.

פֿאָרקער

ר׳ יצחק לוריע, האָט נישט אונטערגע־
שיידט צווישן אָרגאַנישן און אומאָר־
גאַנישן לעבן, נאָר באַשטאַנען דערויף,
אַז נשמות זײַנען פֿאַראַן אומעטום און אַז
פֿאָרקער מיט זיי איז מעגלעך.
— גרשם שלום

אַ דאַנק, זאָגן די שיך,
וואָס דו האָסט אַוועקשטעלט אונטערן בעט.
און אַ דאַנק, זאָגט די קאַלדרע,
פֿאַר דער וואַרעמקייט פֿון דײַן הויט.
אַ דאַנק, זאָגט דער פֿענצטער,
פֿאַרן אונטערהייבן מײַן קוואַטיר.
און אַ דאַנק, זאָגט דער בעזעם,
פֿאַרן אָנהאַלט פֿון דײַנע הענט.
אַ דאַנק, זאָגט דאָס העמד,
פֿאַרן פֿאַרקנעפּלען מיר די אַרבל.
און אַ דאַנק, זאָגט דער סטאַוו,
פֿאַרן וואַרפֿן מיר שטיינדלעך.
אַ דאַנק, זאָגט די בלומען־ציבעלע,
פֿאַרן אײַנפֿלאַנצן מיך אין דער ערד.
און אַ דאַנק, זאָגט די פֿעדער,
פֿאַרן שרײַבן אָט די שורות.
אַ דאַנק, זאָגט דאָס בוך,
פֿאַרן איבערמישן מײַן בלאַט.
און אַ דאַנק, זאָגט דער שפּיגל,
פֿאַר דײַן פּנים יעדן טאָג.
און אַ דאַנק, זאָגט דעלמאָר,
פֿאַרן געדענקען מײַנע לידער.
אַ דאַנק, זאָגט די תּורה,
פֿאַרן זאָגן „שמע ישׂראל!״
און אַ דאַנק, זאָגט דער טאַטע,
פֿאַר דער מתּנה פֿון דײַן לעבן
און די מאַמע זאָגט דאָס זעלבע
פֿון איר קבֿר אין מײַן האַרץ.
און אַ דאַנק, ענטפֿער איך,
בײַ מײַן אַרויסגאַנג פֿון דאַנען —
וווּ איך זאָל נאָר וואַנדערן
באַגלייטסטו מיך אַהין...

Intercourse

*"Isaac Luria did not differentiate
between organic and inorganic life
but insisted that souls were present
everywhere and that intercourse
with them was possible."*
— *Gershom Scholom*

Thank you say the shoes
you have placed under the bed.
And thank you says the quilt
for the warmth of your skin.
Thank you says the window
for lifting my sash.
And thank you says the broom
for the grip of your hands.
Thank you says the shirt
for buttoning my sleeves.
And thank you says the pond
for throwing me stones.
Thank you says the bulb
for my planting in earth.
And thank you says the pen
for writing these lines.
Thank you says the book
for turning my page.
And thank you says the mirror
for your face each day.
And thank you says Delmore
for remembering my poems.
Thank you says the Torah
for chanting the Shema.
And thank you says my father
for the gift of your life
and my mother says likewise
from the grave in my heart.
And thank you I reply
In my exit from here —
wherever I travel
you go with me there.

74

Homage to Dvosye

Remembering Dorothy Bilik (1928-1998)

When I think of Dorothy I think of Brooklyn,
of Flatbush, of Pitkin Avenue, of Eastern Parkway
and the Botanical Gardens, of the Brooklyn Museum
and its Egyptian mummies. I think of *Ich hob der in drerdt*
and *nisht haynt gedact* and *gezinter hayt*. I think
of Brooklyn College, Samuel Gompers, the CIO
and the Internationale, of the New Deal, of the Rosenbergs
Ethel and Julius, of Whittaker Chambers
and Alger Hiss.
                    When I think of Dorothy I think of Proust
stepping, tentatively, off the IRT
at Church Street, looking both ways, perplexed.
It is summer and he is perspiring profusely.
Dorothy appears, takes him by the hand
and guides him to her rooms — Proust falls to the bed
exhausted. "Dvosye," he whispers, "a *bissel* tea, cherie,
avec limon. Deux sucre, and *ruggelach*.
A Sheynem dank." Yes! I can feel the memories —
they come like a flooding of the heart.

When I think of Dorothy, I think of
Wordsworth and Coleridge over a plate
of warm matzoh brie in Grasmere. Coleridge
can hardly contain himself. He is fevered
And in love, once more. *"Dvosye,"* he says,
"Ich hob a poeme far dir."

> *Halt oyf zelbst-umtsutroy*
> *And gib mir a bisl mithilf.*
> *Du bizt a bafligelte Nimfe —*
> *Main tzoyber. Main licht.*

What means this Yiddish, asks Wordsworth, puzzled
looking as always to Coleridge, who translates:

> Suspend your disbelief
> And give me some relief.
> You are a winged sprite —
> My Ariel. My light.

When I think of Dorothy, I think
of Mendele and Peretz and Scholem Aleichem,
of Moshe Kulbach and Itzik Manger
sitting and shouting at each other, eating blintzes
and sour cream and carp and herring, black bread
and olives and cheese. They agree only on Dvosye.

At the next table Bellow and Isaac Rosenfeld,
Malamud and Roth — they cannot make up their minds:
kasha varnishkas or *kishke*, *latkes* or brisket?
Egg beaters, they settle for. *Gevalt*, says Roth
is there a life beyond cholesterol.

Bashevis enters from the kitchen
in his slippers. He is carrying a bowl
of steamed carrots and peas — he winks
at *Dvosye* who is reading Glückel and Kafka
with the Jewish Encyclopedia by her side.

When I think of Dorothy, I think of the *Klezmorim*
playing far into the night, the clarinet kicking in
faster now and faster — Dorothy, her skirts whirling,
wildly as though there was no air to resist her
as though you could not tell the dancer from the dance
as though she took dominion here and there, as though
she was rising now, high and higher into my heart,
her wings opening like Ariel's aloft in flight.
O Dvosye! How bright. How bright.

זְחֵא *Take Hold*

אִם אֵין מְאוּמָה
לְפָנֶיךָ, אֱחֹז
בּוֹ. יִתָּכֵן שֶׁהַמַּזָּל יָאִיר לְךָ פָּנִים
וְיִתָּכֵן שֶׁלֹּא. אַף עַל פִּי כֵן הַנַּח
אוֹתוֹ עָמֹק בְּתוֹךְ כִּיסְךָ.
זֶהוּ נֶכֶס
שֶׁאֵין מִשֶּׁלּוֹ.

If there is nothing
before you, take hold
of it. You may be fortunate
or not. Place it deep
in your pocket regardless.
It is a possession
as no other.

כְּשֶׁאַתָּה חַיָּב לָלֶכֶת וְכָל
נִשְׁלְמוּ; כְּשֶׁמְּצַוִּיםהָכָנוֹתֶיךָ
עָלֶיךָ לְהַכְרִיז עַל כָּל
נְכָסֶיךָ, הַכְנֵס אֶת יָדְךָ
אֶל הַכִּיס הָאָפֵל.

When you are to leave and
have made all your
arrangements; when you
are ordered to declare all
your possessions, reach in
to the dark pocket.

הַנּוֹסֵעַ, זֶה אֵינֶנּוּ
סֵמֶל, אַף לֹא מִצְעָד.
שׁוּם דָּבָר
אֵינוֹ שָׁלֵם כְּמוֹ הֶחָלָל
שֶׁבַּאֲוִיר
אֲשֶׁר אַתָּה חוֹצֶה.
אםוְהוּא שֶׁלְּךָ.
אָכֵן תֹּאחַז בּוֹ.

This is no symbol
traveler, no parable.
Nothing
is as whole as the space
in the air
you pass through.
And it is yours. If
you will take hold of it.

Interlude

Words let water from an unseen, infinite ocean
Come into this place as energy for the dying and even the dead.
— *Rumi*

Ist dir Trinken bitter, werde Wein.
If drinking is bitter to you, turn yourself into wine.
— *Rainer Maria Rilke*

Poetry is not poetry by reason of its content or ambiguity
but by reason of its allowing musical elements (time, sound)
to be introduced into the world of words.
— *John Cage*

The difference between the comic side of things, and
their cosmic side, depends upon one sibilant.
— *Vladimir Nabokov*

You never know what is enough unless
you know what is more than enough.
— *William Blake*

Homage à Beckett

Ever tried. Ever failed. No matter.
Try again. Fail again. Fail better.
    — Samuel Beckett, Worstwood Ho

O! Beckett a bucket full, a mindful
of fouling — sweats & shudders & rages &
O! heart burster   *Mere existence is so much better*
than nothing that one would rather exist
even in pain / said Sam Johnson.
And Raskolnikov: *Man is a vile creature!*
And vile is he who calls him vile for that
And Godot? Where goeth Godot
would she — she! — have said
what's fair if not fear filling — ah! — the air
though thruck in the ear.
                    So at the end
what's to fear? O! Sam Beckett
Fare thee well awhile
& fair winds to you & Malone
alone out there
& O! Molloy *nihil*
No nothing in hell as much of blank
as there is Beckett. *De mortuis nihil nisi bonum*
Of the dead, say nothing but good.

Selah

The Old & the Ne^w

The old sentence, so it's said, is a long freight train
hauling syntactic units across the Plains
getting the old goods* from one place to another,
dependable as the sun's apparent rise gives us morning
and its apparent descent gives us night.
All well and good — God's in his heaven etcetera.
Commerce of all kinds depends on the old sentence: you have
a purchase order, a bill of lading, you can track its shipping
and know its expected time of arrival. You may be satisfied
or not: still, the old sentence got the job done.
All hail the old sentence.
                        Now the new sentence. Ah!
Dependable as (you choose): the weather   sub-primes
Al Qaeda   Congress   taxes   young love
The new sentence   upward   a
                falls   nywhe
                                        re

old goods: lyric I, deep image, epiphanies, vatic, sonnets, sestinas, etc.

and the goods   the new goods**
come
dropping in like para
                    c
                h
                    u
                t
                e
                s

new goods: non-referential, dada, paratactic, clinamatic, collage, zaum, disjunctive, etc.

landing in a line perhaps — perhaps not.
Meaning? A wild surmise
                    Who knows
what happens next
                Cage?   Ives?
Whoops! Sunrise
            SURPRISE!

Mirror

Thank you for giving us
the opportunity
to read your manuscript.

We have considered it
carefully but regret that
we cannot keep the work.

Although we would like to send
an individual response
to everyone, and particularly

to those who request comment
the small size of our staff
prevents such correspondence

Because of the enormous
number of manuscripts
we receive we ask that you

limit submissions to no more
than four poems. We appreciate
your interest in Poetry

Quest

?	?	?	?	?	?	?
?	?	?	?	?	?	?
?	?	?	?	?	?	?
?	?	?	0	?	?	?
?	?	?	?	?	?	?
?	?	?	?	?	?	?
?	?	?	?	?	?	?

~

0	0	0	0	0	0	0
0	0	0	0	0	0	0
0	0	0	0	0	0	0
0	0	0	?	0	0	0
0	0	0	0	0	0	0
0	0	0	0	0	0	0
0	0	0	0	0	0	0

If God Does Not Exist, Everything Is Permitted —
If God Does Exist, Ditto

Golem Gol
em Golem G
olem Golem Go
lem Golem Gol
em Golem G
olem Gole
olem Golem
olem Golem Golem Gole
em Golem Golem Golem Golem G
Golem Golem Golem Golem Gole
Golem Golem Golem Golem Golem Gole
lem Golem Golem Golem Golem Golem Gol
Golem Golem Golem Golem Golem Golem G
m Golem Golem Golem Golem Golem
olem Go Golem
olem Go lem Golem Golem Golem G olem Go
m Golem em Golem Golem Golem Go m Gole
olem G m Golem Golem Golem G olem Go
Golem lem Golem Golem Golem G Golem
em Gole Golem Golem Golem Gol m Gole
Golem m Golem Golem Golem Go em Gol
m Gole Golem Golem Golem Golem Golem
m Gol m Golem Golem Golem Gole Golem
Golem G olem Golem Golem Golem G em Gole
em Golem Golem Golem Gole
olem Golem G em Golem Go
lem Golem Go lem Golem ol
m Golem Gol em Golem Go
lem Golem Go lem Golem G
olem Golem G olem Golem
Golem Golem Golem Gol
Golem Gol lem Golem
lem Golem olem Gole
em Golem olem Gol
m Golem G Golem Go
Golem G lem Gole
olem Gole m Golem
lem Gol em Gole
m Gole m Golem
Golem G olem Gole
m Golem Go lem Golem
Golem Golem Golem Golem
Golem Go lem Gol

85

life is here/is life here
here life is/is here life
life here is/here is life

this is life	*Permutations*	this is death
is this life		is this death
life this is		death this is
is life this		is death this
this life is		this death is
life is this		death is this

death is there/is death there
there death is/is there death
death there is/there is death

Nature and Art

"There is no comfort in nature" — Darwin

the seas the mountains the trees
theseasthemountainsthetrees
heseasthemountainsthetree
eseasthemountainsthetre
seasthemountainsthetr
easthemountainsthet
asthemountainsthe
sthemountainsth
themountainst
hemountains
emountain
mountai
ounta
unt
n

"There is some comfort in art" — Says who?

Ascending and Descending in My Own Backyard

He had a dream in which he saw a stairway resting on the earth
with its top reaching to heaven, and the angels of God
were ascending and descending on it. Genesis 28:13

descending

descending

descending

descending

descending

descending

descending

descending

descending

descending

descending

descending

descending

descending

ascending

ascending

ascending

ascending

ascending

ascending

ascending

ascending

ascending

ascending

ascending

ascending

ascending

ascending

The More Fun House on Porter Street, N.W.

Remembering John Pauker

is burgundy and full of misplaced dreams,
a museum of singing gin and applauding ducks
the ace of spades lounging on the floor sipping
bourbon and ginger ale. Light bulbs are blooming
dark brocades of reason. In one corner Nixon is carefully
painting his fingernails scarlet. Jimmy is picking at his teeth
with a toothpick, and Lyndon — O! Lyndon — is playing
hide 'n seek with a blonde under the bed.
Relax cries the chorus. Place your hands on your heart
and listen for its erratic bliss as though Pagliacci
has burst through the swinging doors. The cobra
in the corner winks its purple eye and commands
the Pharaoh to say, ah, cheese.

> Jelly beans are
a bowl of blinking eyes. Even the windows rise
in welcome. You wander from a Berber village
in one room to a Mongol outpost in another.
On your shoulder a white crow sings O Sole Mio
and eats pistachio nuts while little porkers
gambol over fences counting dreams.

We are at the darkening end of Porter Street
sometime in the 1970s or elsewhere ages hence
where the moon is a great bright plate
and the felon lives — a small impresario in black
polka dot shirt and green striped pants. He is laughing
like a grimace. The naked maja lounges on the chaise
longingly, her sweet tongue and ruby lips
hold your mouth hostage.

> Raising his baton
the jester of sorrow lifts music over the fields of death,
croons to a peacock under blue glass and bows low
to his audience — you and me and all the
rest of us out here applauding in the third row.

Because He Could Not Stop for Death

A full three days of Allen whose conversation could filibuster the sun's descent — and Death's mission as well, which he once did. I was there. Early morning and a rapping at the door that Allen opened with a great toothy welcome. I've been expecting you, Allen said. I know came the reply, that's why I'm here. Is there enough time for a glass of wine, asked Allen? Of course said Death I've waited this long, I'm in no great hurry. And thus Allen began, a soliloquy about Death as the final stage on the journey of life, about Blake on his death bed calming his wife with assurance that dying was simply going from one room to another (albeit the door is locked from behind). About Scheherazade and her *One Thousand and One Nights*, about Ali Baba and the Forty Thieves, and Meher Baba, a manifestation of Jesus himself the Risen Christ, about reincarnation and the many lives ahead of us and behind, about burning the impurities with each successive one, that neither Essence nor Existence precedes the other, about the differences between brain and mind, about what Kierkegaard did not understand, let alone Spinoza and Kant, about Wittegenstein's conclusion to the *Tractatus* — of that which we cannot speak, we should remain silent — and *The Death of Ivan Ilych* and *Our Town* as the twin pillars of literature and life, about human consciousness and James Hillman — hold to nothing and nothing will hold to you — of Jean Gebser and the aperspective, about the ego as steel structure that entraps itself, about the Holy Roman Empire, Shiva, The Jewish Question, the Bronx and the New York Giants — Willie Mays a true mensch — about Louie the Father who would piss on his son's grave (Allen's), and yes! about Eros, the power of women, living without money, the beauty of the marriage of true minds, the dancing Sufis, Rumi, Hafiz, and Blake (again) — Energy is eternal delight. Hours passed through day into night, then another and another. Allen could not stop — Death became heavy lidded, began to loll in his seat, and by day three finally passed out. Allen did not notice. Suddenly a rapping at the door and Death's attendants entered — they lifted him up and carried him to the waiting carriage. We will revive him they said and return tomorrow — please be ready. Allen smiled toothily as they exited — I'll be waiting, he said.

The Republic of Imperishable Lines

To see a world in a grain of sand and a heaven in a wild flower

The world is charged with the grandeur of God

Trailing clouds of glory do we come

For in his morning's orisons he loves the sun and the sun loves him

Exuberance is beauty. Energy is eternal delight

Surely some revelation is at hand

And I am dumb to tell

For he on honeydew hath fed and drunk the milk of paradise

O frabjous day! Callooh! Callay!

Who shall say I am not the happy genius of my household?

Nature never did betray the heart that loved her

Whan in Aprill with his shoures soote

My heart in hiding stirred for a bird —

The achieve of, the mastery of the thing!

That thou light wing'd Dryad of the trees singest of summer in full-throated ease

But at my back I always hear Time's winged chariot hurrying near

The lone and level sands stretch far away

April is the cruelest month, breeding lilacs out of the dead land

A robin redbreast in a cage puts all heaven in a rage

Never again would birds song be the same

They bring the eternal note of sadness in

Bare ruin'd choirs, where late the sweet birds sang

About suffering they were never wrong, the Old Masters

Your ma and pa they fuck you up, they don't mean to but they do

I smiled at him but he stuck out his tongue and called me nigger

Black milk of dawn we drink it at dusk we drink it at noon

They cannot look out far, they cannot look in deep

I shot him dead because, because he was my foe, just so

I learn by going where I have to go

Farewell, thou child of my right hand, and joy

Because I could not stop for Death He kindly stopped for Me

How do you like your blue-eyed boy, Mr. Death?

Life, friends, is boring. We must not say so

I have measured out my life with coffee spoons

When I consider how my life is spent

I'd sooner, except the penalties, kill a man than kill a hawk

I think I could turn and live with animals, they are so placid and self-contained
What did I know, what did I know of love's austere and lonely offices?
I should have been a pair of ragged claws
No memory of having starred atones for later disregard
Send not to know for whom the bell tolls
I have wasted my life
He moves in darkness as it seems to me
Though I sang in my chains like the sea
Argh, we were all beautiful once, she said.
The art of losing isn't hard to master
Not, I'll not, carrion comfort, Despair, not feast on thee
The feelings I don't have, I won't say I have
You see what I am: change me, change me
For christ's sake, look out where yr going
For you as yet but knocke, breathe, shine, and seeke to mend
We will make our meek adjustments
A man's a man for a' that
Whatever lives lives because of the life put into it
The ancient Poets animated all sensible objects with Gods or Geniuses
Each new attempt is a raid on the inarticulate
Till the gossamer thread you fling, catch somewhere, O my Soul
When I have fears that I may cease to be
The nothing that is not there and the nothing that is
The Truth must dazzle gradually
We set up mast and sail on that swart ship.
To follow knowledge like a sinking star
Now I am grateful to my small poem for teaching me this again
Poetry is the supreme fiction, madame
As imagination bodies forth the forms of things unknown
Shine, perishing Republic, *shine on*

III

What I Want of It

I want to find it as though wandering
Perhaps dazed and unaware of itself. It doesn't know
Its own story but awoke in the middle of a poem
Looking for just what, it knew not. Its stories
Are the narratives of its encounters along the way,
In cities among strangers, in rooms teeming with silence,
On suburban streets or at a table on some back porch
That looks out to a forest glistening with mysterious syllables.
Its tales are sagas of fiction that it cannot help telling
Regardless, and with an amazement that all this is happening
To someone, an orphan, who is just now discovering itself
Here, in the moment of telling all this to no one in particular.
What stories! It says in astonishment. Where did they all come from?
And why?

The Past

wasn't always so. It was a white hot
'69 Corvette once or in 1954 a new
T-Bird sleek and ebony passing you
with wild contempt, or even a Kaiser
convertible in 1952, rose-colored
knight of peculiar countenance striding
on Sunrise Highway east towards Montauk
and the sea. Heads turned in strange surmise.

But beauty ages, pal,
and even the best lines go soft, the sweetest body
(let's face it) cannot hold up. Service it
though you will, garage it against life's storms,
follow every precaution — you can never
do enough. Either fatigue finally sets in —
or boredom. Salute their former dignity
or stash them in a museum, or write
encomia remembering them fondly
or sing of glories (like the ancient poets)
that inevitably go to ruin.

You know the course:
the child becomes a man, survives
to three score ten, more or less, and then
becomes a child again, or worse.
Soon he's merely memory and then a blank.
Listen up. The day is calling, and the night.
Damn the cliches. Full speed ahead.
Pull out all the stops. Just drive the poet wrote
into something rich and strange — and keep
the damn thing straight and on the road.

In the beginning was the Word, and the Word was with God, and the Word was God. John 1.1 ¶ Do you think you can teach me with words? Book of Job ¶ Words are the physicians of the mind diseased. Aeschylus ¶ Once sent out a word takes wing irrevocably. Horace ¶ He words me girls, he words me. Shakespeare, Anthony and Cleopatra ¶ These words are razors to my wounded heart. Titus Andronicus ¶ Why should calamity's woes be so full of words. Richard III ¶ My Son, hear My words, for My words are most sweet, surpassing all the knowledge of the philosophers and wise men of the world. My words are spirit, and they are lift and are not to be weighed by man's understanding. They are not to be drawn forth for vain approbation, but to be heard in silence, and to be received with all humility and with deep love. Thomas à Kempis ¶ My Son, stand fast and believe in Me. For what are words but words? They fly through the air, but they bruise no stone. Thomas à Kempis ¶ If words have all their possible extent of power, three effects arise in mind of the hearer. The first is, the sound; the second, the picture, or representation of the thing signified by the sound; the third is, the affection of the soul produced by one or by both of the foregoing. Edmund Burke ¶ Words often understand themselves better than those who use them. Friedrich Schlegel ¶ Great deeds are accomplished, not by feats of arms, but by magical means — by the power of words and incantations. Novalis ¶ We talk about the tyranny of words, but we tyrannize over them too. Charles Dickens ¶ There is no conceivable beauty of blossom so beautiful as words — none so graceful, none so perfumed. It is possible to dream of combinations of syllables so delicious that all the dawning and decay of summer cannot rival their perfection, nor winter's stainless white and azure match their purity and their charm. Thomas Wentworth Higginson ¶Every word we speak is million-faced or convertible to an indefinite number of applications. Ralph Waldo Emerson ¶

Words

At any moment and with no warning
they will slip in or come crashing through —
when you are driving between work and home
or struggling in a drowned sleep trying to pull
yourself up from an undertow tugging you down
like the angel of death.
There you are trapped
in the mirror brushing your teeth
or washing your hands and of a sudden they are here
at your door having broken past the gates of civility,
legs kicking and fists pounding — the need is on them.
What else can it be?

           You might have a houseful
of guests or be deep in meditation. They barrel on
through and would blow your house down.
Come on goddamn you they cry *come now. Now*

You reading or hearing this will understand.
Manic one moment, sulking the next,

Writing was what he lived for, lived by, lived in. The word was the light, the word was the church, and the word was now. Alfred Kazin on Henry David Thoreau ¶ Nothing would induce me to lay down my pen if I feel a sentence — or even a word ready to my hand. The trouble is that too often — alas! I've had to wait for the sentence — for the word. Joseph Conrad ¶ Words and magic were in the beginning one and the same thing, and even today words retain much of their magical power. Sigmund Freud ¶ I ought to be able to invent words capable of blowing the odor of corpses in a direction other than straight into mine and the reader's face. Franz Kafka ¶ The epidemic sickening of the word in our time, by which every word is at once covered with the leprosy of routine and changed into a slogan. Martin Buber ¶ What is the man is his way of using words, his sensibility. Max Jacob ¶ Spells and incantations, what we call magic words, the sacred language of paganism . . . are rows of mere syllables which the intellect can make no sense of, and they form a kind of beyond sense [zaum] language in folk speech. Nevertheless an enormous power over mankind is attributed to these incomprehensible and magic spells, a direct influence upon the fate of man . . . The magic in a word remains even if it is not understood and loses none of its power. Velimir Khlebnikov ¶

Words ought to be a little wild, for they are the assault of thoughts on the unthinking. John Maynard Keynes ¶ I would rather have been a painter than to bother with these goddamn words. William Carlos Williams ¶ There is nothing, no, no, never nothing, / Like the clashed edges of two words that kill. Wallace Stevens ¶ Words and words and words, how they gallop — how they lash their long manes and tails. Virginia Woolf ¶ It is among the consequences of or perhaps one of the conditions for the very existence of words, that they eye can tell us the truth, that they can lie to us … and that they can do whatever they are doing in the poems we have been looking at. William Butler Yeats ¶ Words is like the spots on dice: no matter how you tumbles them, there's times when they just won't come. Jean Toomer ¶ Where I go, words carry no weight: it is best, then, I surrender their fascinating counsel to the silent dissolution of the sea which insures nothing because it values nothing. W.H. Auden ¶ I can love things but I cannot love words — they have no hardness, no colors, no taste. Herman Hesse ¶ The Germans even forbade us to use the words "corpse" or "victim." The dead were blocks of wood, shit, with absolutely no importance. Nothing. The Germans made us refer to the bodies as "Figmen," that is, as puppets, dolls or schmattes. Shoah ¶ Words strain, crack and some break, under the burden, / under the tension, slip, slide, perish, / Decay with imprecision, will not stay in place, will not stay still. T.S. Eliot ¶ We're smothered by words, images, and sounds that have no right to exist, coming from, and bound for, nothingness. Federico Fellini ¶ Many a single word also itself is a concentrated poem, having stores of political thought and imagery laid up in it. F.J. Phelps Richard ¶ What I like to do is to treat words as a craftsman does his wood or stone or whatever have you, to hew, carve, mould, coil, polish and plane them

they will beseech and promise you anything —
incantations to raise the dead, blessings
for the evening meal, the lush prose of seduction,
proclamations calling for peace or war.
*We are at your service, aides-de-camp when you reach
out to the enemy — there is no loyalty like ours* they say
(nor betrayal you think). *We want only to serve.*
You want too much I say but then
just when I give in and am counting on them
they turn away — abruptly. *Exhaustion* they say
from having been called on too often to marvel
at wings fluttering in lamplight or to grieve
over a child's murder at its mother's hand
or to sing out at the winds knocking on your window
or settling its palms on your lover's breast.

        And yet

turn away as they inevitably will, they will return
still again when you have given up and least expect them.
Open the book of your heart I have heard them whisper
in moments of calm

        and we will be there.

into patterns, sequences, sculptures, fugues of sound. Dylan Thomas ¶ They lift our spirits — these poor weak words. They guide us and they coerce. They settle fights, initiate disputes, compound errors, elicit truth. How long have we known it? They gather dust, too, and spoil in jokes which draw our laughter like the flies. William Gass ¶ To arrest once and for all, the meaning of words — that is what Terror wants. Jean-Francois Lyotard ¶ It is difficult to put into words what I suffered. Kay Redfield Jamison ¶ Words are our most inexhaustible source of magic. J.K.Rowling ¶ It is hard to trust words, or indeed to know what words actually mean. Judith Butler ¶ The remoteness of words from suffering. Christopher Hill ¶ The word, whether spoken or printed, represents a power greater than that of the atom. … He who has articulated a word has accomplished a Deed. He has taken all the power and responsibility on himself. He is dangerous. He is free. He is destructive. He is God's rival. Tatyana Tolstoy ¶ One must be chary of words because they turn into cages. Viola Spolin ¶ Too often our words weight us down like unremembered dreams. David Appelbaum ¶ In the end Yossel Birstein whispered to his daughter: "Words, words, words… and more words." Clive Sinclair ¶ Don't give us poems of unspeakable lives / if you can't make the words bleed. Madame Red

Butterflies by Brookside

American Painted Lady
Anessa virginiensis

Cabbage White
Pieris rapae

Clouded Sulphur
Colias philodice

Comma
Polygonia c-album

Great Spangled Fritillary
Speyeria cybele

Grey Hairstreak
Strymon melinus

Monarch
Danaus plexippus

Mourning Cloak
Nymphalis antiopa

Pearl Crescent
Phyciodes tharos

Rear Admiral
Pyrameis atalanta

Red-Spotted Purple
Limenitis arthemis

Silver-Spotted Skipper
Epargyreus clarus

Spring Azure
Celastrina ladon

Tiger Swallowtail
Papilio glaucus

Question Mark
Polygonia interrogationis

Northeast Kingdom

. . . they talk of hallowed things, aloud —
and embarrass my Dog.
                    — Emily Dickinson

Walking 122N — Glover to Sheffield
memorizing poems by Du Fu
amidst the peeps and cheeps
                    of a sudden
                                        whoooosh
and buttercups and lilac-scented air hmmmm
                                        and
breaks from the high grass —
                    a red-winged black one
riffling (stream) clover ferns maples
                              ruff ruff
piss hits dry grass — and
                    Shush. Keep still
You've said
          too much already. Enough.

Resemblances

And here on the left hand
is what he is
and there on the right
is what he would be.

The left hand often
loses its way
falters where it would step
is continually in debt, misses
deadlines, apologizes too much, lies
like an alcoholic, worries
the dot over every i, must squint
to see clearly
wakes to a despair so deep down
light finally gives up
and goes home.

The right, on the other hand,
is impatient with such indirection
knows the value of money
pays its bills on time, owes
nothing to the government, never
gets fines, is as reliable
as death, has a clean house,
new furniture, gives *tzedakah*
each day, dresses well
and has plaques on its wall
for community service.

The left hand sometimes
fights with the right
not in street brawls
but as if over a word in midrash
or like a husband and wife
of long years or a shopkeeper and
customer over the price of

damaged goods. This is all right
I say for us out here:
it is good theater and gives
us something to gossip about or make art from.
Meanwhile the left hand sleeps
with the peace of mountains and
the right with the worry of storms.
Who can explain life's inexplicable ways?

⁓

Every so often calm descends
between mountain and storm, and it is then
you invite yourself in, a visitor
carrying candies and cakes. On such days
the right hand takes hold of the left,
and both sit over steaming hot glass of tea
dropping sugar cubes in. And like ancient
antagonists who have grown old together
they sip at the tart bitter sweetness until dark.

Breakfast

Remembering William Stafford

This morning I'll skip the bacon
and eggs and have a poem over light —
two or three if you don't mind.
I feel my appetite coming on.
And even a stack of flapjacks
which I love — with butter
and boysenberry jam spreading
their fingers of sweetness over
the ragged edges — won't do me now.
When this hunger's on, only a poem
will do, one that will surprise my need
like a stranger knocking
at the door (a small knock — at first,
I hardly hear it) to ask directions,
it turns out, to this house. He's looking
for me. Who are you I ask? Your brother
he says, the one you never knew you had
or the one who you've been trying to remember
all your life but somehow couldn't recall
until now, when he arrives. And there he is
before me smiling, holding out his arms
— and all this by chance. Do you
believe it?
          So serve me up a poem friend,
but just go easy on the tropes,
for instance, synecdoche and such. A simile
or two is fine and metaphor's all right.
A rhyming quatrain, maybe on the side
would be ok, but not too much —
they sometimes give me gas.
God I love a breakfast such as this.
It gives me a running start and keeps me going
through to dark when I'm as hungry as a horse.
But that's another poem. Let's eat.

Frühstück

Heute morgen verzichte ich auf Speck und
Eier, zugunsten eines leight gegarten Gedichtes —
auch zwei oder drei, wenn's recht ist.
Ich fühle meinen Appetit schon wachsen.
und selbst ein Stapel Pfannkuchen,
die ich liebe — mit Butter und
Boysenbeermarmelade, die ihre Finger
klebriger Suße uber abgerissene Rander
spreizt — kann mich nicht locken.
Wenmn ich solchen Hunger hab, muss ein Gedicht
her, eines, das mich in der Not überrascht
wie ein Fremder, der an die Tür
kloopft (ein leises Klopfen — anfangs,
kaum zu hören), um nach dem Weg zu fragen,
und wie es sich herausstellt, zu diesem Haus. Er sucht
mich. Wer bist du, frage ich? Dein Bruder,
sagt er, von dessen Existenz du nicht wusstest,
oder an den du dich dein Leben lang erinnern
wolltest und irgendwie nicht wusstest,
oder an den du dich dein Leben lang erinnern
wolltest und irgendwie nicht konntest,
bis jetzt, da er gekommen ist. Und da steht er
lächelnd vor mir, streckt seine Arme aus
— und all dies zufällig. Kannst du
es glauben?
              Also serviere mir ein Gedicht, mein Freund,
aber bitte schone mich mit Tropen, zum Beispiel,
mit Synecdochen und Ähnlichem. Ein Vergleich
oder zwei sind gut und eine Metapher wird geduldet.
Ein reimender Vierzeiler, vielleicht als Beilage,
wäre prima, aber nicht zu viel —
manchmal erzeugen sie Blähungen.
Oh Gott, wie ich solch ein Frühstück liebe.
Es gibt mire den richtigen Anstoß und hält mich auch
im Dunkeln aufrecht, wenn ich Hunger habe wie ein Pferd.
Aber das ist ein anderes Gedicht. Lasst uns essen.

Translated into German by Sabine Pascarelli

Under a Full Moon at Midnight

This is a paean to relief and ecstasy.
A man's poem of course — the electric ah!
in the long stream arcing a rainbow
under the spotlight moon, a covenant between
my body and the earth's.
                          I think of Li Po smiling
silently on Green Mountain and can hear Rumi
drunk on rapture — drink my brother he calls to me,
think of the elephant loosening a great ebullient
stream that floats a river past your house and drops
turds so immense you could build a hut from them
along the shore to shelter your children.
                                What release!
Think of your child pedaling under your hand
and of a sudden — it just happens — you let go
and he's off on his own, free for that first time —
the achieve of, the mastery of the child.
See the stalwart trees in their silence
the stones resting in the driveway, the cat curled asleep
on the front porch, the smear of blood
on the lion's mouth sitting over his fresh gazelle
the morning paper and its stories shouting
for attention. The plenitude of it all.
                                And perhaps
somewhere a friend is dreaming of me, or someone
a stranger is peeing ecstatic under the same moon.
A covenant then between us.
                        True or not. It is no matter.

Morning Talk in the Branches

Wake early and you will hear
the first tentative risings,
the single notes lifting one by one
out of their dark moorings
as if once more they have given in
either to their unsurety or amazement,
like yours, at the darkness again
loosening itself and giving way
as though drapes were opening
to the slow rising overture
of light.

Don't think that I believe
these voices come in praise
as heralds to the new light
or that their sweet sounds
lift light out of some somber home
or that there is any more here
than my need, and perhaps yours
for giving.

They are here, simply. Like
the dark underground rivers
moving slowly, deliberately beneath
your feet or the involuntary rush of blood
sounding noiselessly through your body
or the snows that drift down under
inevitable law, or the tide flooding
and ebbing twice each day.

I know, and you as you must,
that they have their voice and we ours.
Yet still if we listen closely as though their calls were
an ancient memory, you may hear
the language of return, how dark turns to light,
light to dark, how the sea and the sky
must inevitably meet — all those beginnings and ends
returning once more to themselves.

105

Nature

As much a harridan driven by rage
as a Lilith of the renegade need
or dewy-eyed Eve fluttering her lids
and baring her seductive breasts.
It is whatever you would make of her.
Or call her a him with his murderous
battering of outraged jealousy
or, suddenly, sweet disposition
as though leaf-filled and dressed out
in sweet fragrance, a great rooted tree
the central calm of our lives, or as quickly
and without warning the tearing
apart of flesh on the hard floor of the savanna
or storm after storm ripping apart shore and trees.
The new news is the old news —
Nature is all service to need, yours and mine.
It is a palette for signifying
the heat between your legs or the fever in your soul
or the madness of your heart. It is a vast
untamed dictionary for the chop chop
of noun, verb, object and ancillary hangers on,
a murmuring of sentences longing for a home
as though there were small islands to rest on
or easy waters to swim in
or unbounded air to fly above the mind's fevers
in ascent and down and up again.
Tell it that way or however you can.
Nature may simply be a cistern to drink from,
or a seven-course meal to stuff yourself on
or a ripe pear that after a long night's thirst
fills your mouth with nectar and promise
and sweetness of satisfaction and calm.
Ah! you say to yourself: you have returned
from a desert and you are whole again.
You are whole again.

Two Conjunctions and a Pronoun

And

the beauty of this morning for example
the fog supine and hovering over the pond's surface
drifting as in a slow public dance amidst a steady
breeze, the aromatic brew of newly ground
coffee steaming through these rooms, the thrum
of hummingbird wings and the proboscis sipping
on the nectar of nasturtium in the window box before me —
and flying in, red-winged blackbirds, a blue jay
two jet crows lording it over the cut grass
here and in all the garden round and a chipmunk
slipping into the bird feeder my two friends deep
in sleep in separate rooms, the surround of silence
the pen's nib making its way across the lined
surface leaving words in its wake.
                                    It is time to leave
the Kingdom where we've settled in for months
amidst each day's scent of cow pies wafting on
the wind or rising on the back of the afternoon heat
and the sky wide open in this amphitheater
of cumulus clouds grazing like herds and....

Or

Turn words into a carnival of handstands and
holy imaginings.
— Rabbi Avital of Zaragosa

So this a.m. the poem must choose whether
to go into hiding or camp out in bear country
and hunt big game, or be angry and depressed
at its desk, or seek relief in the welcoming arms
of Eros or argue with itself over the worth of poetry
anyway or search the web for ways
to heal its hemorrhaging 401K or plead its case
in language court — it did not come to a glottal stop
as it should have — or go to the Asian market
for ripe fruit and lemons that will singe the tongue
and send shivers of current through the body
or dine with the ghost of Sholem Aleichem —
I tell you it is an ugly and mean world and only to spite it
one mustn't weep! If you want to know, the true cause
of my constant good spirits, my so-called humor — not to cry
out of spite! Only to laugh out of spite, only to laugh —
or rattle on against imperialism, ours and everyone else's,
or read *The Nation* on corporate corruption yet again
the plight of illegals, and the meanness abroad
and in America amidst the idolaters of dogma —
or maybe wrestle an old poem and pin it finally
to the page — or sit down to a three-egg omelet
with feta and bacon, home fries and thick slices
of salty lox, a slather of cream cheese and bagel,
or perhaps, yes! the poem should simply go back to bed
under a down quilt and slip into a dream of lines
galloping over the prairies or flying in on carpets
from Istanbul — they are delivering all manner
of urgent messages. If only I understood Turkish.

The Indefatigable It

It is everywhere and potentially
The basis of being, a form of non-structured
Structure that will inspire a great deal of trust
If you allow yourself to trust It.
Everyone has the capacity to know It.
While many emphasize the absence of It
Once you have accepted and internalized It
It will coalesce into a vision.
It offers a uniqueness. In the beginning
It was quite small.
                    No more. It can prevail
But It is up to you. It can make or break
An organization, a community,
Even a country. While you can take courses in It
The learning that characterizes It
Can only come through action on behalf of It.

It seemed to happen like this:
It is a hard morning bright and chilly.
Maybe she is frightened by It.
It all happens with lightning speed.
The camera moves from his eyes to that pullover
So that we can see a red stain on It.
He lifts her up from the floor — but already he
Is too late. I can feel It under my fingers.
The camera returns to It several times.
It is clear that this meeting is their first.
In other circumstances you might call It a cry, a howl.
But now It is only the sound of emptiness.
It has lasted three minutes. That's It.
We remember It all. We start to believe It is our role.
Slowly, and without noticing It, a hardness creeps over and into us.
The close-up is one scene too many because It is senseless.
It all speaks to our amazement, and we are fastened to It.

Old Shoes

The ones resting in a corner
worn, flaccid, deep-furrowed —
once babyskin sleek, twin jaguars
that stalked the night
two cruise ships plowing head-on
through stormy seas, steady
amidst all.
        O welladay! old shoes
of mine. Time now I suppose
for the sad shoe grounds.
You who served so well —
your former grace still shines through
but it's time to go old shoes
and like Mr. Black I'm feeling the blues.

Sparrow

Learn about pines from the pine,
and about bamboo from the bamboo
— *Matsuo Basho*

Here at the window's ledge, opposite me,
a sparrow's pecking for crumbs that I'd not seen.
OK I say (to myself), you are there on one side
of the divide and I am here on the other.
You are under the high blue and I, under
a low ceiling — I am pecking too.

It is clear what you're after. What of me?
Perhaps I want to celebrate you, sparrow
there on that other side and out in the high blue.
Maybe I'll go on to compare your ordinariness
with mine, your small brown wings
and my lack of them.
                    I don't know yet.

So for our different reasons here we sit
each of us feeding ourselves, you on crumbs,
me on words. What are mine wanting? Perhaps
to be a sparrow, for now at least, nothing more.
Perhaps they want to sail aloft without thinking,
to sit under the sky's spring blue, then with little
effort rise high heigh-ho
and soar over the earth's green furze below.

Ah!

> *A single one of her smiles would perturb*
> *the whole city of Yang and derange the*
> *suburb of Hsia-ts'ai.*
> *— Sung Yü (third century B.C.E.)*

There are some faces
that put all others to shame. Yours.
They cry out for eternal fidelity.
for avowals of forever, until death
do us part, there's no other but you.
Listen, we're not innocents here,
you know as I do these avowals
are heat and desire going hard for you.
Beneath this camouflage of syllables
Rises an involuntary lust.
Come, let us.

Fruit

For Ann

It is my desire for fruit, you es-
pecially, your tart pulp jibbing
my taste your rich
smell running windward on
my tongue curved like
a spinnaker its taste full of
seed splitting the curve
of the rind breaking
fruit. Your taste   the
quince and green space and
marvel of tartness.
                    Says the
goat laughing   friend, it's the high blue
and spring

The morning sparkles like lemons
and I carry home the
gifts of seed   apples   figs   pears
especially pears pregnant
seedy   full   that
the tongue licking a jug of honey
rocks in delight with and
oranges and grapes purpling
lips and a man who
cares for the deep yellow   who
loves the feel
the firm and the round of a pear and eats

A Suite

1.
My wife says
You should take better care of your feet.
Look at those poor dawgs:
Hammer toes, bunions, corns, neuromas. Ugh!
What neglect they have suffered.
Think of the abuse they have carried you through
running up and down courts, climbing mountain
after mountain of despair, then descending
deeply into valley after valley of the same.
The least you could do is give them the care
they so richly deserve: warm baths to begin with,
unguents, soothing creams and a loving woman — honey on her tongue —
to lay next to.

2.
I'm sorry
I'd like to help
but I'm not going
to keep your
feet warm.
I'll knit you
a pair of socks.

3.
What I know of Rabbi Weiss of Bilke
though it would not fill a shot glass, is this:
to study Talmud into the night, he'd stick his feet
in ice water and keep them there, it was said,
to ward off sleep from spreading through his body.
I have it on no authority, of course, but I would like to think
it was his way to not forget his body while his soul
set forth into the thick wilderness of God's law.

O! Rabbi Weiss of Bilke, not even a smudge in my memory
not a pinprick in the history of the dead,
I can imagine you at Matisse's table, the light
holding you in place, dining on the sweet breath of life,
old men wringing from each hour the honey that flows like fire
in the blood.
                Rabbi Weiss of Bilke, for godsake,
who knows how you might have forsaken your wife for study,
or for that matter how you came to her in dark passion,
your appetite for wisdom, like Solomon's, so full
you met each other with gratitude and love.

O! Rabbi Weiss of Bilke, I drink to the memory of your feet —
may they live in incandescence to light
even the darkest way.

Late Afternoon Light

What is wanting here in this late afternoon? The sun in its apparent move down and its horizontal light gives to this pen a momentary glint, the fan laboring in the worst monotony that we might ever imagine for ourselves, and the accompanying slight breeze, the full curve of the body pregnant, the daisies ebullient yellow and wild carrot in the earthen vase taking the small winds, and the page as if in lift rising and I know that this is the intrusion of mind — to accept all that is given. Thus the apple core going to brown, the new infant, the shadow leaning its darkness on your hand, the single leaf, the blind glare, the extraordinary exactness of anything — as temporary as it will be, and gone, in this recognition. That is all and everything, the wanting to be so far into love, there is no light lead you out.

Morning — Early Summer

It's not that I love this early morning
light that begins its glimmer between
these close houses anymore than I do
the high bright glare of noon or the sun's
last light that drowns in swales of orange over
the farthest edges of the city.

It is only that here, in the momentary
silence, before the glimmerings step fully
out from the borders of darkness — the rooms
filled with silence, palpable, your body in sleep upstairs,
the birds not yet claiming their territory —
I am breathing beneath the earth's dark skin,
tuned to all the invisible respiration
chugging like engines out in the backyard
                                        full, complete,
at no odds with the darkness there or with the constant
feeding and being fed upon, a calm,
every need quiescent, still, ready
for whatever will come on and however
and the heat that will soon lay down its steamy paws
over each and every thing living and dead.

The Hidden Life

has been so long hidden it is dead
it thinks. The hidden life wants desperately
to reveal itself, wants to speak candidly,
wants to shout without thinking, wants to meet you
unexpectedly coming around a corner
on the East Side maybe or along a country road
in the Northeast Kingdom, anywhere, startled
as a child with its first taste of the sea.
And the hidden life cries out, yes, it is you
of course, where were we that we had not met
before and cries out, again, it is you
I was just now desiring so.
                            The hidden life
is up now, is taking two steps at a time
chasing you, is running to keep up,
is dancing on a crowded street with you
is growing wings lifting you
from the ground, is soaring with you
in astonishment and looking down
upon the earth's slumbers.
                            And the souls
of the dead stand up in applause —
even the minor gods look on
unable to contain their joy.
And you return once more, together
naked in the light, having buried
the hidden life, having risen once more
from the land of the dead.

Rains

1.

For two nights and one long day, the rains
have not stopped. They have drenched the earth,
have made a sponge of it, have left the foliage
leaden with wet, leaves adrift and capsizing,
this back field an ocean of grass.
You can feel your own self dragged under and
down, struggling to pull yourself up.
And still through this rising flood
what manner of birds sounding their calls
through the sopping rain? Neither heartbreak nor
heart's love in them. Nor promise nor grief
nor courage, nor giving up.
                              And here you are
emptied out over love — its loosening
its drift and departure.

2.

Of course they are singing whatever
we need them to sing. Resist. Hold out.
This too will pass. We will forage again.
We will feed our young. Listen to these
choruses of no expectation
with their empty syllables echoing
yours.
            If the sun stays dark today, it will
break through tomorrow or the day after.
It does not matter. Your body for some
unaccountable reason rises
on these notes like a well made boat
riding the cliff of storm-driven waves
that would drag you under for good.
And yet you ride their lift with no
expectation, just trust. All that they are
is all that they are. And for now that is enough.

פֿריי זיך   *Rejoice*

וואָס האָט די וועלט צו טאָן מיט דיר?
אָדער דיר אָדער מיר? וואָס קען עס ארן די צײַט,
די אומבאַרירלעכע אַבסטראַקציע?
אָדער די לבֿנה, די זון, די שטערן
אָנגעזעװדיקע און אומזעיקע? אָדער דעם אָקעאַן
וואָס פֿלייצט צו צו דײַן טיר? אָדער דעם גרויסן דעמב
אין דרויסן וואָס שאָטענט דײַנע געדאַנקען?
אָדער די פֿינקען וואָס שפּײַזן זיך פֿון זוימען
אויסגעשפּרײטע פֿון דיר? אָדער די בערג
ניט צו באַרויִקן הינטער דיר? אָדער זכרונות
וואָס האָבן אָפּגעלאָזט זייער אָנהאַלט — אונדזער מאַמע
אין ווײַטן האָריזאָנט, דײַן טאַטע און אַלע
וואָס האָבן דיך געהאַלטן און געצערטעלט מיט
ליבעוװערטער פֿון אָנהייב אָן? אָדער, זאָג עס, דאָס לעבן
וואָס האַלט נישט קיין טרויער און נישט קיין גליק
סײַ בײַ דײַן קומען, סײַ בײַ דײַן אַוועקגיין? אָדער די
ערד וואָס וועט דיך צודעקן? אָדער דאָס פֿינסטערניש
וואָס וועט צונויפֿנעמען דײַן שטויב
אָדער די ווינטן וואָס מעגן דיך אויפֿהייבן
און צעטראָגן וווּהין עס זאָל נישט זײַן — צום ים
צום ברעג ים, אין די בערג, די וועלדער,
ווידער אַ מאָל צו דער ערד?

פֿריי זיך. פֿריי זיך.

What has the world to do with you
or you or me? What can Time
that unassailable abstraction care?
Or the moon, the sun, the stars visible
and invisible? Or the ocean
rolling in at your door? Or the great oak
outside that shades your thoughts?
Or the finches feeding on seeds
you have set out? Or the mountain
implacable behind you? Or memories
that have given up their hold — your mother
in the far horizon, your father and all
who have held you and spoken love to you
from the beginning? Or, say it, this life
which holds neither grief nor happiness
in your coming or in your going. Or the earth
that will cover you? Or the darkness
that will gather your dust to itself
or the winds that may lift
and scatter you anywhere — the sea,
the sea's edge, the mountains, the forests,
the earth once more?

Rejoice. Rejoice.

Beginnings and Ends

Here is the word
That divides the dark
And here is the word
That is filled with light

Here is the word
That severs the sea
And separates sky
And uncovers the earth

Here is the word
That revels in breath
And here is the word
That cleaves your soul

And here is the word
For singing your love
And here is another
For singing your grief

Here are the words
That will blind your eyes
That will freeze your tongue
That will strike you deaf

And here is the word
To open the dark
And here is another
To empty the light
And here is the last
To carry you home

Notes

Memory. The quotations around "Memory" and "Words" (p. 96) take their impetus from the Talmud, where an excerpt of biblical text is surrounded on all four sides by commentaries and interpretation.

Heart of Darkness. Reading Richard Holmes's *The Age of Wonder: How the Romantic Generation Discovered the Beauty and Terror of Science* long after this poem found its way into being, I came across following lines: "His heart was a terra incognita quite as mysterious as the interior of Africa."

Montaigne & Me. The following excerpt from Michel Montaigne's (1533-1592) essay, "That to Philosophize is to Learn to Die" — on the hazards of death lurking everywhere — gives a taste of his style, the piling of one example after another. "To omit fevers and pleurisies, who would have imagined that a Duke of Brittany should be stifled to death in a crowd as the Duke was, at the entry of Pope Clement into Lyons? Have you not seen one of our kings killed at a tilting? And did not one of his ancestors die by colliding with a hog? Aeschylus, threatened with the fall of a house, stayed out in the open to no purpose; behold him knocked on the head by the roof of a tortoise falling from the talons of an eagle flying in the air! Another died of grape-seed; an emperor, by the scratch of a comb in combing his head; Aemilius Lepidus by stumbling over his own threshold; and Aufidius through bumping against the door as he entered the council chamber; and between the thighs of a women, Cornelius Gallus the praetor, Tigillinus. . . .

The Hebrew alphabet serves Hebrew and Yiddish, as it does other Jewish languages, for example, Judeo Spanish (Ladino) and Judeo Italian. To the non-reader of these languages, the translations into Hebrew of "A Short History" (p. 41) and "Take Hold" (p. 77) by Moshe Dor and into Yiddish of "Intercourse" (p. 74) and "Rejoice" (p. 120) by Herman Taube are indistinguishable.

Poems by Eytan Eytan. Eytan (1940-1991) grew up among the hills of the Lower Galilee. A graduate of the military high school in Haifa, he was a naval commando. His experience of war's brutality is inseparable from his life as a farmer who tilled the earth and trusted in its fecundity — this dual sensibility is evident in much of his work, from subtle love poems to the intensely powerful "Children/Yeladim," fervently anti-war, desperate in its anguish, incantory, and, finally, transcendent. Like all poets writing in Hebrew, his work cannot help but allude to the Bible. Some are inescapably familiar and will resonate with many readers, for example, in Genesis 25:26, "grasp another's heels" (Jacob and Esau). But there are the not-so-familiar allusions as in, "What says the speaker/ Or even the righteous/ a bald one and she-bears/ None have survived": this refers to Elisha in Kings II:24 and evokes the speaker's rootedness in ancient traditions. Moshe Dor and I edited a special issue of *Shirim* with our translations of Eytan Eytan's poems.

Performance. David Foster Wallace's story "Good Old Neon" works this theme: "Pretty much all I've ever done all the time is try to create a certain impression of me to other people. Mostly to be liked or admired. It's a little more complicated than that, maybe. But when you come right down to it it's to be liked, loved. Admired, approved of, applauded, whatever." *Oblivion: Stories, 2004.*

Struttin'. Takoma Park, Maryland, commissioned a bronze statue in its city center of a rooster, Roscoe, who in the 1980s held dominion of Carroll Avenue, the main street. I wrote "Roscoe of Takoma Park" as a homage — originally titled "Roscoe Magnus," it was part of the annual urban poetry walk, posters designed by students at Montgomery College for the now-annual Spring for Poetry in Takoma Park. Posters can be found at the website of the Friends of the Takoma Park Maryland Library, www.ftpml.org. "Cocka Doodle Do" is the prequel.

Dismantling. An observation by Marjorie Perloff may have led to this poem: "Like Rimbaud, William Carlos Williams must break down all cultural and natural forms, kill everyone, and destroy everything in order to return things to the primal chaos from which a reality without any antecedents may spring. . . . Once this monstrous act of demolition has been satisfactorily completed, the world will be new, and the imagination can turn from acts of destruction to acts of authentic creation." *The Poetics of Indeterminacy.*

Limits. The golem is a life-sized figure formed from clay and brought to life by Kabbalistic or mystical incantation. Though the word first appears in Psalms, its modern folklore derives from 16th century Prague. No Jewish folktale has inspired so much in the way of literature and art.

Abraham Avinu, Our Father Abraham. Abraham, descended from Shem, Noah's son (Genesis 11:10-32 and 14:13), is the forefather of Judaism, Christianity, and Islam. While Judaism and Christianity are rooted in the Ibrahim-Isaac line, Muslims believe Muhammad, the founder of Islam, is descended through Ishmael.

Abraham and the Binding of Isaac. In Hebrew, the binding of Isaac is called the Akedah, a story central to what became Judaism and Christianity. On the Jewish New Year (Rosh Hashanah), morning services, always include the Torah portions on the birth of Isaac and the Akedah (Genesis 21 and 22). I have drawn upon several translations: *The Torah — A Modern Commentary*, ed. W. Gunther Plaut; *The Five Books of Moses — A Translation with Commentary* by Robert Alter; *The Five Books of Moses — A New Translation with Introductions, Commentary, and Notes* by Everett Fox; *Pentateuch and Haftorahs*, ed. Dr. J.H. Hertz; *King James Bible*; *Rashi — The Sapirstein Edition*, trans. Rabbi Yisrael Isser Zvi Herczeg. Of the 34 English translations of Gen. 22 that I have searched, only four translators account for the Hebrew *kach na*, "take, pray": Robert Alter, Everett Fox, Young's *Literal Translation*; Rabbi Herczeg translates *kach na* as "please"; all the other translations use the imperative "Take." According to the *Hebrew and English Lexicon of the Old Testament* (Oxford, 1907, 1968 reprinted with corrections), the Hebrew *na* (nun aleph) is an "entreaty or exhortation . . . rarely [used] in a command." The line could be construed to read that Abraham had the choice to refuse — *kach na*, "take, pray."

Sarah. Midrash (plural, Midrashim) derives from the root meaning, "to study," "to investigate"; midrashim are Jewish commentaries or elaborations — legends, parables, exegeses — of incidents in the Bible that aim at providing a moral lesson.

If God Does not Exist, Everything Is Permitted — If God Does Exist, Ditto. The first part of this quote is given feverish voice by Ivan in Dostoevsky's "The Grand Inquisitor," *The Brothers Karamazov*.

Words. As in the poem "Memory," the idea for surrounding quotations derives from the commentaries in the *Talmud*.

Resemblances. The epigraph by Carl Jung is from *Man and His Symbols*. If two epigraphs were not so cumbersome, I would have used this from Thoreau's *Walden*: "Do not let your left hand know what your right hand does, for it is not worth knowing."

Mark the Music is typeset in Granjon, 11 over 14.
Granjon is an old style serif typeface designed by
George William Jones (1860-1942) in the period 1928-1929.
The roman version is based on a font from Claude Garamond,
and the italic version on one from Robert Granjon,
both typefaces used in a book published in 1592.
Mark the Music is printed on acid-free papers by
McNaughton & Gunn, Inc., Saline, Michigan.